Louise Emma Potter
Ligia Lederman

Atividades com música para o ensino de inglês

DISAL
EDITORA

"What's wrong with the world, mama?"
Black Eyed Peas

"Tonight's the night the world begins again."
Goo Goo Dolls

"Your faith was strong but you needed proof."
Leonard Cohen

"Imagine people sharing all the world."
John Lennon

"I don't wanna drink again, I just need a friend."
Amy Winehouse

"We don't need no education."
Pink Floyd

"I dreamed that love would never die."
Les Misérables

"Like a candle in the wind
Never fading with the sunset."
Elton John

"Our friendship will never die."
Toy Story theme

"You make me smile like the sun."
Uncle Kracker

"What do you feel when you see all the homeless on the street?"
Pink

"He said each day's a gift and not a given right."
Nickleback

"Have you come here for forgiveness?"
U2

"You always taught me right from wrong."
Madonna

© 2013 Louise Emma Potter e Ligia Lederman

Preparação de texto
Gabriela Morandini / Verba Editorial

Capa e projeto gráfico
Paula Astiz

Editoração eletrônica
Laura Lotufo / Paula Astiz Design

Assistente editorial
Aline Naomi Sassaki

Dados Internacionais de Catalogação na Publicação (CIP)
(Câmara Brasileira do Livro, SP, Brasil)

Potter, Louise Emma
    Atividades com música para o ensino de inglês / Louise Emma
Potter, Ligia Lederman. -- Barueri, SP : DISAL, 2012.

    Bibliografia
    ISBN 978-85-7844-124-1

    1. Ensino – Materiais didáticos 2. Inglês – Atividades, exercícios
etc. 3. Inglês – Estudo e ensino 4. Música I. Lederman, Ligia. II.
Título.

12-12445   CDD-420.7

Índices para catálogo sistemático:
1. Inglês : Atividades com música : Estudo e ensino   420.7

Todos os direitos reservados em nome de: Bantim, Canato e Guazzelli Editora Ltda.

Alameda Mamoré 911 – cj. 107
Alphaville – BARUERI – SP
CEP: 06454-040
Tel. / Fax: (11) 4195-2811
Visite nosso site: www.disaleditora.com.br
Televendas: (11) 3226-3111

Fax gratuito: 0800 7707 105/106
E-mail para pedidos: comercialdisal@disal.com.br

Sumário

Introdução

A sala de aula de Língua Estrangeira (LE) mudou. Precisamos ir além do ensino das estruturas gramaticais não contextualizadas. Devemos envolver nossos alunos e expô-los a diferentes gêneros que estão presentes no seu cotidiano, trazendo essa realidade para a sala de aula. Por meio da música podemos abordar temas transversais, aprender sobre as questões da vida real e suas transformações.

Como professoras de inglês, percebemos a necessidade de desenvolver meios mais próximos da realidade dos alunos para atingir objetivos linguísticos e pedagógicos. Dessa forma, podemos motivar os alunos a participar mais ativamente da aula e aprender de maneira mais prazerosa.

O objetivo deste livro é orientar professores de inglês a preparar e utilizar atividades com música para complementar o ensino na sala de aula.

O livro é dividido em duas partes: na primeira encontram-se as atividades fotocopiáveis para os alunos; na segunda há informações sobre o autor, cantor ou banda; orientações para o professor; respostas das atividades e as letras completas das músicas.

As atividades foram divididas em dois grupos: o primeiro contém atividades mais curtas para serem usadas no início de uma aula como *warm-ups*, ou no final da aula, para revisar conteúdos ou verificar a aprendizagem. O segundo contém atividades planejadas para uma aula de cinquenta minutos.

As atividades estão divididas por níveis: básico, pré-intermediário, intermediário e avançado. Antes de cada grupo de atividades, as músicas estão organizadas em quadros para facilitar a escolha daquela que se adapta melhor ao perfil da sua classe.

Como todo professor sabe, o planejamento é um passo de extrema importância para que o resultado seja positivo. É importante ler com atenção as orientações para o professor para compreender os objetivos sugeridos. Apresentamos neste livro ideias para planejar e tornar a sala de aula um ambiente de interação e aprendizagem de LE mais motivador.

"Música é a linguagem universal da humanidade"
Henry Wadsworth Longfellow (poeta americano)

Por que usar música?

A música oferece uma mudança de rotina na sala de aula de LE. Ela oferece recursos para que os professores possam desenvolver com os alunos as quatro habilidades: *listening*, *speaking*, *reading* e *writing*. Como dito por Lo e Fai Li (1998: p. 8), aprender inglês usando música expõe os alunos, que normalmente sentem certa tensão ao serem expostos a uma língua estrangeira, a um ambiente seguro e não ameaçador de linguagem autêntica.

Dois estudos, Domoney e Harris (1993) e Little (1983), investigaram a prevalência da música popular na vida dos alunos aprendizes de LE. Esses dois estudos demonstram que a música é a maior fonte de inglês fora da sala de aula. A exposição à linguagem autêntica de forma divertida estimula a aprendizagem dos alunos.

Vejamos alguns bons argumentos para usarmos música em sala de aula:

- Músicas em inglês fazem parte do cotidiano dos nossos alunos. Eles as ouvem com frequência fora da sala de aula.
- As músicas sempre contêm linguagem autêntica. Porém, os professores devem ser cuidadosos ao escolher a música a ser utilizada. Há músicas que contêm palavras e conteúdos inadequados.
- Há uma gama enorme de músicas que podem ser escolhidas de acordo com o perfil e idade dos alunos.
- Há uma variedade de vocabulário, conteúdo, pontos gramaticais, temas e aspectos culturais que podem ser abordados em uma única música.
- Por meio de músicas os professores podem desenvolver o senso crítico dos alunos.
- Podem-se usar as músicas como *warm up*, como o tema principal da aula ou como verificação de aprendizagem.
- Os alunos podem ser expostos a uma variedade de sotaques diferentes do inglês e, por meio de músicas de diversas origens regionais, serem apresentados a culturas diferentes.
- As músicas retratam o mundo atual, portanto, com as letras das músicas o professor pode explorar situações da atualidade.
- Música relaxa, diverte e ensina.

Como planejar as atividades de música

Before the class

- Existem diversos gêneros de músicas que podem ser utilizados para preparar as atividades: *reggae, rock, country, romantic, pop, blues, jazz...* E muitos clipes estão disponíveis no YouTube.
- É importante conhecer o perfil de seus alunos antes de escolher a música que será utilizada. Converse com eles para descobrir suas preferências e escolha com cuidado. Dessa forma, os alunos serão motivados e estimulados a aprender.
- Certifique-se de que haja uma relação entre o conteúdo da música e o objetivo pedagógico do curso em andamento. O tópico que está sendo apresentado em sala de aula deve ter uma relação direta com a atividade de música que você desenvolverá.
- É importante que a música seja apropriada para a faixa etária do seu grupo de alunos. Por exemplo: ao abordar temas polêmicos na letra da música, certifique-se de que seus alunos têm maturidade para discutir o assunto.
- Escolha a música relacionada ao seu objetivo. É essencial que você escolha cuidadosamente a música que será utilizada de acordo com o nível linguístico dos alunos. Eles até podem ser expostos a uma linguagem mais elaborada, porém a atividade proposta deve ser possível de ser realizada.
- Ouça a música e certifique-se de que tenha entendido plenamente todo o vocabulário.
- Prepare atividades variadas que possam ser desenvolvidas durante o período de uma aula. (Lembre-se de que os alunos ouvirão a música mais de uma vez.)
- Confira se o equipamento a ser usado está funcionando e disponível.

During the class

- Devemos ter o cuidado de enfatizar o objetivo que queremos alcançar. Lembre-se de que essas atividades são complementares e proporcionam a oportunidade de rever conceitos gramaticais e conteúdos lexicais, além de desenvolver competências estratégicas de forma motivadora. Isso deve ser explicitado aos alunos por meio de instruções claras, antes da atividade.

- Ao iniciar a atividade de música, devemos ativar o conhecimento prévio dos alunos através de perguntas sobre o tema/título da música. Observe como isso é feito nas atividades apresentadas neste livro.

- Utilize estratégias para desenvolver a acuidade auditiva dos alunos, caminhando do mais geral para o mais específico, de maneira gradativa. Por exemplo, ao propor uma atividade, podemos pedir que os alunos prestem atenção somente à melodia, solicitando que tenham como foco o tipo de música (reggae, rock, romântica etc.), os instrumentos usados, o número de pessoas que está cantando, o tom da voz, ou seja, tópicos mais gerais. Em seguida, as perguntas podem ser mais específicas.

- Desenvolva atividades de pronúncia enfatizando as rimas contidas na música.

- Desenvolva atividades de vocabulário com o objetivo de apresentar vocabulário novo e reforçar vocabulário conhecido, além de propor que deduzam o significado de palavras novas através do contexto apresentado.

- Reforce o entendimento do uso de tópicos gramaticais apresentados em sala de aula. Use o contexto para que os alunos reconheçam esses tópicos na música e em seguida os utilizem.

- Desenvolva atividades de leitura utilizando as letras das músicas. Se o objetivo for desenvolver estratégias de leitura, apresente somente as letras e desenvolva atividades sem o som.

- Exponha os alunos às variedades da língua inglesa e também às diferentes culturas dos países onde se fala inglês. Podemos escolher músicas nas quais as pessoas sejam de diferentes regiões desses países. Podemos apontar os diferentes sotaques e regionalismos e os temas que estão sendo abordados.

- Estimule a criatividade por meio do uso de insumos visuais, apresentando o videoclipe da música sem o som. Dessa forma, os alunos têm a oportunidade de levantar hipóteses sobre o tema, levando em consideração somente a imagem do clipe.

- Desenvolva o senso crítico dos alunos por meio dos temas polêmicos escolhidos e, ao mesmo tempo, possibilite o debate e revisão de valores.

After the class

- Elabore perguntas aos alunos sobre as atividades apresentadas. Dessa forma tanto os alunos quanto o professor se conscientizarão sobre os objetivos alcançados.
- Proponha atividades extraclasse relacionadas com o objetivo linguístico escolhido. Por exemplo, uma atividade escrita: ouvir a música em casa e escrever a respeito da mensagem do compositor.

Como conduzir as atividades de música

Before Listening

Escolha até dois dos tópicos abaixo:

- Estimule o **conhecimento prévio** do aluno fazendo perguntas relevantes a respeito do tópico. Desenvolver atividades de *lead in* é muito importante para baixar a ansiedade dos alunos, pois atividades de *listening* são consideradas difíceis.
- Elabore o **levantamento de hipóteses** a respeito do **título** da música.
- Faça as atividades de **reconhecimento** ou **expansão de vocabulário**, e o *brainstorming* de palavras que podem aparecer na música.
- Levante hipóteses a respeito do **tópico da música** escrevendo algumas palavras-chave na lousa e pedindo que os alunos imaginem qual tema será abordado durante a música.
- Mostre o **videoclipe** da música sem som e pergunte aos alunos qual é o tema da música.
- Dê aos alunos algumas estrofes e peça a eles que deem um **título** para cada uma delas.
- Dê uma atividade de relacionar as estrofes com **títulos** dados por você.

Listening

Apresente aos alunos tarefas com objetivos específicos.

- Reconhecer vocabulário.
- Reconhecer o sentimento expressado na música: tristeza, melancolia, saudades, crítica política etc.
- Reforçar estruturas gramaticais: reconhecimento e uso dos tempos verbais.

- Elaborar questões de múltipla escolha ou perguntas e respostas.
- Ordenar estrofes, versos ou palavras.
- Utilizar o videoclipe como *input* para a escrita: os alunos devem escrever um roteiro relacionado com o tema ou fazer um resumo depois de ouvir e ver um trecho da música.
- Assistir ao videoclipe sem o som. Em seguida peça-lhes que ouçam a música e pergunte aos alunos se o tema da música está relacionado com o clipe ou peça aos alunos que criem uma estória sobre a música.
- Completar sentenças, relacionar colunas, atividades de Verdadeiro ou Falso, justificando-as.
- Sublinhar palavras cognatas, sinônimos, antônimos, *exponents*, modais, respostas específicas, etc.
- Classificar, organizar e ordenar vocabulário.
- Reconhecer rimas.
- Realizar *brainstorming* de palavras semanticamente similares.
- Reconhecer versões diferentes da mesma música. Pergunte qual o aluno prefere e por que. Aponte as diferenças de sotaque e de gênero musical.

After listening

- Peça aos alunos que escrevam um pequeno texto a respeito da música, relatando suas impressões pessoais sobre o tema.
- Peça aos alunos que relatem outras músicas sobre o mesmo tema.
- Apresente aos alunos vocábulos embaralhados usados na música e peça que desembaralhem e formem sentenças com eles.
- Peça aos alunos que usem expressões que apareçam na música em sentenças.
- Faça as atividades gramaticais usando o tópico gramatical que aparece na música.
- Peça aos alunos que mandem suas impressões sobre a música por alguma rede social usando *I think* _____ *because* _____ .
- Crie um *blog* para que os alunos postem as impressões deles sobre a música.

Atividades de música

Parte 1

Vinte atividades fotocopiáveis de 20 minutos

	Música	Cantor / Grupo	Tema	Nível
1	"Everything"	Michael Bublé	Love	Basic
2	"Imagine"	John Lennon	Peace, war, poverty and government	Basic
3	"You've got a friend in me"	Randy Newman	Friendship	Basic
4	"Ebony and ivory"	Paul McCartney and Stevie Wonder	Prejudice and racial integration	Basic
5	"Somewhere only we know"	Keane	Secret places	Basic
6	"Gotta be"	Des'ree	Motivational	Pre-intermediate
7	"Listen to your heart"	The Maine	Teenage love	Pre-intermediate
8	"Better days"	Goo Goo Dolls	New Year Resolutions and Christmas	Pre-intermediate
9	"Rehab"	Amy Winehouse	Addiction	Pre-intermediate
10	"I don't wanna miss a thing"	Aerosmith	Love	Pre-intermediate
11	"Come home soon"	Corey Crowder	Loved ones	Intermediate
12	"Another brick in the wall"	Pink Floyd	Education	Intermediate
13	"Earth song"	Michael Jackson	Environment	Intermediate
14	"Into the West"	Annie Lennox	Death	Intermediate
15	"What kind of world do you want?"	Five for fighting	World consciousness	Intermediate
16	"Crying shame"	Jack Johnson	War	Intermediate
17	"That I would be good"	Alanis Morissette	Being positive in spite of adversities	Intermediate
18	"Colors of the wind"	Disney	Environment	Advanced
19	"The living years"	Mike and the Mechanics	Generation gap	Advanced
20	"Vienna"	Billy Joel	Time issues	Advanced

Everything

Michael Bublé

Disponível em: http://www.youtube.com/watch?v=SPUJIbXN0WY

Acesso em: 23/07/2012

Before listening

1. Complete the sentences with the words below. Use the context. Check with a partner.

true – car – day – well – do – say – bell – far – carousel – you

You're a falling star, you're the getaway _____.
You're the line in the sand when I go too _____
You're the swimming pool, on an August _____
And you're the perfect thing to _____.
And you play it coy but it's kind of cute
Ah, when you smile at me you know exactly what you _____
Baby, don't pretend that you don't know it's _____.
'cause you can see it when I look at _____.
You're a _____, you're a wishing _____,
And you light me up, when you ring my _____.
You're a mystery, you're from outer space,
You're every minute of my everyday.

Listening

1. Listen to the song and check your work.

2. Listen again. Write down 5 positive words or expressions you hear in the song. In pairs, think of 5 words with negative meanings related to them.

POSITIVE	NEGATIVE

After listening

1. Write four sentences. Two of them using positive words from the song and two of them using negative words.
2. Match the expressions to their meanings in Portuguese according to the context. Check with a partner.

a) a falling star   ( ) poço dos desejos
b) the getaway car   ( ) estrela cadente
c) play it coy   ( ) carro em fuga
d) kind of cute   ( ) você me faz lembrar
e) you ring my bell   ( ) fazer-se de boba
f) a wishing well   ( ) engraçadinha
g) don't pretend   ( ) Espaço sideral
h) outer space   ( ) não finja

Imagine

John Lennon

Disponível em: http://www.youtube.com/watch?v=yRhq-yO1KN8

Acesso em: 23/07/2012

Before listening

1. Work in pairs. Write four sentences about what your perfect world would be like. Use:

a) In my world there is _____.
b) In my world there are _____.
c) In my world there is no _____.
d) In my world there are no _____.

2. Share your ideas in groups of four students.

Listening

1. Listen to the song and complete the sentences. How did Lennon imagine his perfect world? Check in pairs.

a) There's _____, _____ and _____.
b) There's no _____
_____ no _____
there's no _____
no _____
no _____

2. Listen to the song again and find three different pairs of rhymes.

a) _____ / _____
b) _____ / _____
c) _____ / _____

After listening

1. Write a sentence about your impressions of the song and post it on your favorite social network. Use:

   I think "Imagine" by John Lennon is _____ *because*
   _____ .

2. Listen and find the opposite words in the song. Make a sentence with them. Show them to a colleague.

   Below _____
   Easy _____
   Live _____
   War _____
   Generosity _____

3. Sing together.

You've got a friend in me

Randy Newman

Disponível em: http://www.youtube.com/watch?v=zB2gPZRsz0Q

Acesso em: 23/07/2012

Before listening

1. Read these words and discuss with your group what/who they remind you of?

**empathy – friendliness – attachment – affinity – bond – harmony – intimacy
affection – trust – rapport – relationship – love – acceptance – companionship**

2. Watch the video (no sound). What is it about?

3. Answer these questions individually and check in pairs.

    a) Do you have good friends?
    _____

    b) Do you have a best friend? Who is she/he?
    _____

    c) What's your friend like? Describe his/her personality.
    _____

    d) Can you describe him/her physically?
    _____

    e) Do you have a friend who's not a human being?
    _____

Listening

1. Listen and order the stanzas:

( )
But none of them will ever love you the way I do
It's me and you
And as the years go by
our friendship will never die
You're gonna see
It's our destiny
You've got a friend in me
You've got a friend in me

( )
When the road looks rough ahead
And you're miles and miles
From your nice warm bed
Just remember what your old pal said
You've got a friend in me
You've got a friend in me

( )
You've got a friend in me
You've got a friend in me

( )
Some other folks might be
A little bit smarter than I am
Bigger and stronger too
Maybe

( )
You've got a friend in me
You've got a friend in me
You've got troubles, well I've got 'em too
There isn't anything I wouldn't do for you

We stick together and we see it through
You've got a friend in me
You've got a friend in me

2. Listen and write the comparative forms of the following words. Use them in a sentence describing and comparing two famous people.

Big _____
Smart _____
Strong _____

After listening

1. Write words that start with the letters of the word FRIEND.

F_____
R_____
I_____
E_____
N_____
D_____

Ebony and ivory

Paul McCartney e Stevie Wonder

Disponível em: http://www.youtube.com/watch?v=PSvnIwg0lEA

Acesso em: 23/07/2012

Before listening

1. Based on the verses below predict what the lyrics of the song will be about.

   Ebony and ivory live together in perfect harmony
   Side by side on my piano keyboard, oh lord, why don't we?

   _____

2. What do ebony and ivory refer to in these verses?

   _____

3. Complete the chart by answering these questions: Where are racism and prejudice more evident in the world? Where is racial integration more evident in the world?

RACISM/PREJUDICE	RACIAL INTEGRATION

4. Do you believe there is good and bad in everyone?

Listening

1. Listen to the first stanza. Write the verbs you hear. In which tense were the lyrics written?

   _____

   _____

2. Sit in pairs. Listen again and find words that rhyme with:

   a) harmony: _____ / _____
   b) keyboard: _____
   c) live: _____
   d) know: _____

3. Give the opposites of these words. Find them in the lyrics.

   bad: _____
   dead: _____
   take: _____
   none: _____
   apart: _____
   nowhere: _____

After listening

1. Write four sentences using some of the verbs you found in the present tense.

   Do _____ ?
   _____ not _____ .
   She _____ .
   Does _____ ?

Somewhere only we know

Keane

Disponível em: http://www.youtube.com/watch?v=Oextk-If8HQ

Acesso em: 23/07/2012

Before listening

Answer these questions in pairs.

1. Do you have a place where you like to go and be alone? Describe this perfect place.

2. Are there different places you like to go with different people? Justify.

3. Think of the perfect place for each situation:

   a) To go out with friends
   b) To go out with your boyfriend/girlfriend
   c) To go out with your parents
   d) To have a business meeting

Listening

1. Listen to the first two stanzas and do the following activities.

   a) Extract all the verbs in the past.

_____

b) Extract all the rhyming words.

_____

_____

c) Describe the place where he is.

_____

_____

2. Find rhyming words in the song for the words below. Write them beside the words. Check with a friend.

a) meat: _____

b) case: _____

c) mend: _____

d) worth: _____

After listening

1. Fill out the chart below:

somewhere	everywhere	anywhere
someone		
sometime		
something		

2. Sit in pairs. Make a sentence using each word above. Make sure you use them correctly.

You gotta be

Des'ree

Disponível em: http://www.youtube.com/watch?v=JhpZfltbnAQ

Acesso em: 23/07/2012

Before listening

1. Read the verses. Talk to a partner and discuss what the song is about. Give a title to it.

_____

Listen as your day unfolds,
Challenge what the future holds,
Try and keep your head up to the sky.

Listening

1. Listen to the song and complete the verses with the adjectives you hear.

You gotta be _____   You gotta be _____
You gotta be _____   You gotta be _____
You gotta be _____   You gotta be _____
You gotta be _____   You gotta be _____

2. In two of the examples above there are two comparatives. Which are they?

a) _____

b) _____

3. Read these words out loud, listen to the song and find rhyming words.

a) cheers: _____ / _____

b) my: _____ / _____

c) lace: _____ / _____

d) led: _____ / _____

e) molds: _____ / _____

After listening

1. Write sentences using these adjectives in the comparative form.

a) bad: _____

b) calm: _____

c) hard: _____

d) cool: _____

e) bold: _____

Listen to
your heart

The Maine

Disponível em: https://www.youtube.com/watch?v=RbFc_vAEgIQ

Acesso em: 23/07/2012

Before listening

1. Talk to a partner about these questions.

    a) Do you think there is a perfect age to fall in love?
    b) Have you ever fallen in love? How old were you? How old was he/she?
    c) How did your parents and friends react at the time?
    d) What did they say? Did you listen to them?

Listening

1. Listen to the song and check True (T) ou False (F). Justify using the verses.

    a) Your father thinks you are soul mates.
        ( ) _____
    b) Your mother thinks it's temporary.
        ( ) _____
    c) You should listen to your friends.
        ( ) _____
    d) You should not listen to your heart.
        ( ) _____

2. Read these words out loud. Complete the chart with rhyming words you hear in the song.

line		
smart		
proud		
she		

After listening

1. Exchange ideas about the theme of the song with a partner and then write a paragraph about it.

_____

_____

_____

_____

_____

_____

2. Watch the video clip and sing together.

Better days

Goo Goo Dolls

Disponível em: http://www.youtube.com/watch?v=i-kHIeNYIDc

Acesso em: 23/07/2012

Before listening

1. Answer these questions and check in pairs.

    a) Do you make plans for the New Year?
    b) Do you evaluate your previous year achievements?
    c) Tell your partner 2 things you did last year and 2 things you are planning to do next year.

Listening

1. Listen to the song and mark True (T) or False (F). Correct the false sentences.

    a) No one is forgiven now.
    ( ) _____
    b) Tonight the world ends.
    ( ) _____
    c) Everybody should have a sophisticated place to live.
    ( ) _____
    d) You can give faith, trust and peace.
    ( ) _____

e) You can say a prayer to the poor children.

( ) _____

2. Match the words that rhyme.

**year – live – loud – tonight – clear – strings –
fight – now – give – things**

Listen to the song and clap your hands every time you hear the words above.

3. Does the song make any reference to Christmas? Justify.

_____

_____

4. What do the singers want for Christmas? Quote the verse.

_____

_____

After listening

Write two sentences.

a) about your plans for next year

_____

_____

b) about what you want for Christmas

_____

_____

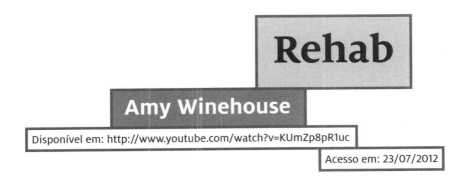

Rehab

Amy Winehouse

Disponível em: http://www.youtube.com/watch?v=KUmZp8pR1uc

Acesso em: 23/07/2012

Before listening

1. What does addiction mean? What different kinds of addiction do you know?

2. Read the first two stanzas of the lyrics of Rehab and answer the following questions.

   a) Why doesn't she want to go to rehab?
   b) What's her father's opinion?
   c) How long should she stay at rehab? What expressions does she use to refer to it?
   d) Where would she rather be?

3. Discuss with a partner the meaning of the phrases "I've been black", "a shot glass", "I'm on the mend" based on the context.

Listening

1. Complete with the words that rhyme.

   a) know: _____ / _____
   b) time: _____ / _____

c) Ray: _____

d) friend: _____

e) class: _____

f) dried: _____

g) here: _____

After listening

1. Fill in the chart with examples of the verb tenses in the song.

SIMPLE PAST	PRESENT PERFECT

2. Write a paragraph about Amy Winehouse using some of the verbs above.

_____

_____

_____

_____

_____

_____

I don't wanna miss a thing

Aerosmith

Disponível em: http://www.youtube.com/watch?v=SWd73bK9-zc

Acesso em: 23/07/2012

Before listening

1. Can rock music be romantic? Give examples of some romantic rock music you know.

2. Do songs always use the correct grammar? If not, give examples.

3. Look at the title of this song. Is there anything wrong grammatically?

Listening

1. Listen to the song and extract all the verbs he uses in the *ing* form.

2. Use the verbs and write something about your routine.

3. Listen again and write the verses where he expresses his deep love for her.

After listening

Wanna and gonna are frequently used in speech in informal colloquial English, mainly American English, instead of want to and going to.

1. Can you think of other verbs which are also used this way in informal speech?

   _____

   _____

2. Make up three sentences and talk to a partner using these verbs.

   _____

   _____

   _____

Come home soon

Corey Crowder

Disponível em: http://www.youtube.com/watch?v=mWX2iFEQjWs

Acesso em: 23/07/2012

Before listening

1. Ask your partner these questions.

   a) Do you listen to music? How often?
   b) What kind of music do you like?
   c) Who's your favorite singer?
   d) Do you like country music?
   e) Do you like songs about love?

2. Complete these sentences.

   a) Love is _____ .
   b) I can't live without _____ .
   c) I miss _____ .
   d) My life is _____ .
   e) There is something _____ .
   f) There is nothing _____ .

3. Share the sentences above with a partner. Choose one sentence and share it with your class.

Listening

1. Find the rhyming words in the song. Add an extra one.

behind			
may			
bride			
spring			
sheep			

2. Listen to the song and find related words.

tomorrow				

3. Listen to the song again and find opposite words.

with	
shallow	
low	
outside	
different	
there	

After listening

1. Complete these sentences. Be coherent.

   a)   I can't bear _____

   b)   I could swear _____

   c)   There is a time to _____

   d)   I've found that _____

   e)   I've refused to _____

2. Share the sentences above with a partner. Choose one and share it with your class.

Another brick in the wall

Pink Floyd

Disponível em: http://www.youtube.com/watch?v=YR5ApYxkU-U

Acesso em: 23/07/2012

Before listening

1. What is your opinion about the school system in our country?

2. How was the relationship with your teachers when you were at school?

3. Do you think Education in schools has changed in the last twenty years? Is it better or worse? Why?

Listening

1. Listen to the first part and fill out the chart according to the title of each column. Check with a partner.

WORDS RELATED TO SCHOOL	WORDS RELATED TO PEOPLE

2. Listen to the second part of the song. Do you agree with what they are saying? Why or why not?

3. Discuss in pairs. What does "Another brick in the wall" mean to you?

After listening

1. Together with a partner think about all the adjectives or words you can use to describe a school.

2. Think about an ideal school. Write about it in the space provided below. Describe it to your friends.

_____

_____

_____

_____

_____

_____

Earth song

Michael Jackson

Disponível em: http://www.youtube.com/watch?v=HNa_r92tdTM

Acesso em: 23/07/2012

Before listening

1. Write down five words that come to your mind when you think about our EARTH.

_____

2. Do you think we take care of the Earth?

3. Think about four actions we can do to help the Earth.

4. Make sentences with the following words thinking about the Earth and its environment.

sunrise – rain – tears – dying – dreams – children – animals – crying – joy – yesterday

_____
_____
_____
_____
_____

Listening

1. Watch the video clip. What comes to your mind?

2. Listen to the song and clap your hands when you hear the words from activity 4 of the before listening task.

After listening

1. Write a paragraph using at least five words you mentioned expressing the meaning of the song.

    _____

    _____

    _____

    _____

Into the West

Annie Lennox

Disponível em: http://www.youtube.com/watch?v=JgcoBKWTW14

Acesso em: 24/07/2012

Before listening

1. Read the first stanza. What do you think this song is about? Exchange ideas with a partner.

   Lay down your sweet and weary head
   The night is falling
   You have come to journey's end
   Sleep now and dream of the ones who came before
   They are calling from across the distant shore.

2. Read the lyrics and underline other sentences that convey the same idea.

Listening

1. Write three words related to LIFE and three related to DEATH you hear in the song. Add another which is not in the song.

   Life _____ / _____ / _____ / _____
   Death _____ / _____ / _____ / _____

2. Listen to the song again. Classify the verbs you hear according to the tenses. Complete the chart.

PRESENT CONTINUOUS	SIMPLE PAST	PRESENT PERFECT	IMPERATIVE	FUTURE
is falling			lay down	will see

After listening

1. Choose two words and two verb tenses from the activities above. Write two sentences about life and death.

_____

_____

2. Explain the lyrics in your own words.

_____

_____

_____

_____

What kind of world do you want?

Five For Fighting

Disponível em: http://www.youtube.com/watch?v=FlYLIZ5RVdw

Acesso em: 24/07/2012

Before listening

1. What kind of world do you want? Sit with a partner and make a list of the perfect world.

_____

_____

_____

_____

_____

_____

Listening

1. Listen to the first stanza. What came in the package he received?

_____

_____

_____

2. Listen to the whole song. Does it mention anything from the list you wrote? Write them below.

_____

_____

_____

3. Rewrite the verse where the singer asks us to begin building our world.

_____

_____

_____

4. List three words he says that refer to nature or nature's destruction.

_____

_____

_____

5. Listen to the song and complete the sentences with the correct verb.

a) _____ a chance

b) _____ a piece

c) _____ a masterpiece

d) _____ your army

e) _____ the other way

f) _____ anything

g) _____ the oceans

After listening

1. Why does he say: "Be careful what you wish for"?

_____

_____

_____

2. Think about five things that can change the world from now on (positive or negative).

_____

_____

_____

_____

_____

_____

Crying shame

Jack Johnson

Disponível em: http://www.youtube.com/watch?v=GN6JyI2tIAg

Acesso em: 24/07/2012

Before listening

1. Talk to a friend. List some of the great causes of wars.

2. Do you think wars will ever be extinct?

3. If you were a president, would you send your people to war? What would you do?

Listening

1. Listen to the lyrics and check True (T) or False (F). Justify using a verse.

    a) ( ) He thinks we communicate well.

    _____

    b) ( ) It is difficult to control the world now.

    _____

    c) ( ) He believes someone wins and someone loses.

    _____

    d) ( ) War uses fear as fuel.

    _____

    e) ( ) There is no one to blame.

    _____

2. Find a verse with the same meaning as the following sentences.

a) People should learn to talk to each other.

_____

b) We are all the same.

_____

c) People will go to war but will not come back.

_____

d) We could try to ignore it.

_____

e) The more people are afraid, the more they fight.

_____

f) Do we know who we are?

_____

g) How will this finish?

_____

After listening

1. Do you believe there is a way to end wars forever?

_____

2. Why is this song called *Crying shame?*

_____

That I would be good

Alanis Morissette

Disponível em: http://www.youtube.com/watch?v=RUaC1nH6Y4U

Acesso em: 24/07/2012

Before listening

1. Classify these adjectives into the categories below.

**miserable – heartbroken – down – hopeless – pathetic – cheerful –
happy – depressed – fortunate – lucky – sad – pleased – walking on air –
on cloud nine – flying high – unhappy – sorry**

POSITIVE MEANING	NEGATIVE MEANING

2. Read the questions below. Discuss with a partner using the adjectives above.

   a) What makes you feel good? What makes you feel bad?
   b) How do you feel when you gain weight?
   c) How do you feel when you break up with your boyfriend/girlfriend?
   d) How do you feel when you are sick?
   e) How do you feel when you lose money?
   f) How would you feel if you won in the lottery?
   g) How do you feel when you fall in love?

Listening

1. Listen to the first stanza and write at least two conditional sentences you hear.

   _____

   _____

2. Underline the verbs in the *if clauses* from the activity above. What verb tense is being used? Write another conditional sentence using this verb.

   _____

   _____

3. Listen to the second stanza, talk to a partner and rewrite it in a positive way.

   _____

   _____

After listening

1. Match the sentences according to their meaning.

   a) I numb myself.   ( ) I was rejected.
   b) I was fuming.   ( ) I feel indifferent.
   c) I was clinging.   ( ) I was very angry.
   d) I got the thumbs down.   ( ) I was holding tight.

   Complete these sentences.

   a) I would be good even if I _____ .
   b) She would be great if she _____ .
   c) If they _____ I would feel miserable.
   d) I would _____ when I _____ .

2. What do you think the composer is trying to express in these lyrics?

   _____

   _____

   _____

Colors of the wind

Disney

Disponível em: http://www.youtube.com/watch?v=TkV-of_eN2w

Acesso em: 24/07/2012

Before listening

1. Do you like cartoons?

2. List some of your favorite cartoon songs and exchange ideas with your friends.

3. Look at the title of this song. What do you think it will talk about?

4. Do you know anyone who was brought up in a completely different culture than your own?

5. Is there right from wrong in this case? Give examples to a partner.

6. Read the stanza below and explain the meaning to your partner.

   You think the only people who are people
   Are the people who look and think like you
   But if you walk the footsteps of a stranger
   You'll learn things you never knew, you never knew

7. Do you believe we are connected to nature? If so, in what way?

Listening

1. Sit in pairs. Listen to the first four stanzas. Give an appropriate title for each one.

    _____

    _____

    _____

    _____

2. State two things Pocahontas is asking John Smith if he has ever done.

    _____

    _____

    _____

3. Complete the verses:

    a) Can you sing _____ ?
    b) Can you paint _____ ?

4. Listen to the song and find the two verses where Pocahontas says we are all connected to each other.

    _____

    _____

    _____

After listening

1. Talk to a partner. Make a list of five things you can do to protect our environment.

    _____

    _____

    _____

    _____

    _____

2. Write a paragraph about your interpretation of the stanza below.

You think you own whatever land you land on
The earth is just a dead thing you can claim
But I know every rock and tree and creature
Has a life, has a spirit, has a name

_____

_____

_____

_____

_____

_____

The living years

Mike And The Mechanics

Disponível em: http://www.youtube.com/watch?v=z8mPS0-2Xq8

Acesso em: 24/07/2012

Before listening

1. Check True (T) or False (F) individually. Compare your answers with a partner. Do you have the same opinion?

a) ( ) A difference in values, beliefs and interests between two different generations is called generation gap.

b) ( ) The generation gap is specially felt when you are a teenager and your parents are in their 50s.

c) ( ) Differences between generations have been increasing in the 21st century.

d) ( ) Different age groups working together can cause a big problem.

e) ( ) Generation X (baby boomers) and generation Y have the same characteristics.

Listening

1. Listen to the first stanza. Rewrite it in your own words.

_____

_____

_____

2. Listen to the second stanza. What happened to his father?

_____

_____

3. Listen to the chorus. Write it below. Discuss the meaning with your partner.

_____

_____

_____

_____

4. Listen to the song. List the words you hear that have positive and negative meanings.

NEGATIVE	POSITIVE

After listening

1. Read the last stanza. Underline the verbs in the past tense.

I wasn't there that morning
When my father passed away
I didn't get to tell him
All the things I had to say.
I think I caught his spirit
Later that same year
I'm sure I heard his echo
In my baby's new born tears
I just wish I could have told him
In the living years.

2. Complete these sentences with your own words.

    a) I wasn't there when _____

    b) I didn't get to _____

    c) I think I _____

    d) I'm sure I _____

    e) I wish I could have _____

Vienna

Billy Joel

Disponível em: http://www.youtube.com/watch?v=oZdiXvDU4P0

Acesso em: 24/07/2012

Before listening

1. Check True (T) or False (F) related to your own reality.

    a) ( ) Twenty-four hours a day are enough for me to accomplish what I have to do.
    b) ( ) I am never in a hurry.
    c) ( ) I am not an ambitious person.
    d) ( ) I take one day at a time.
    e) ( ) I am not a very patient person.

2. Compare your answers with a partner. Are you more relaxed or more anxious than your partner?

3. Match the expressions to their meanings.

    a) slow down   ( ) settle down
    b) cool it off   ( ) embark on
    c) burn it down   ( ) gain ground
    d) get ahead of yourself   ( ) diminish
    e) kick it off   ( ) break down

4. Choose three expressions from the activity above. Write sentences using them. Look at the lyrics to understand the meaning if necessary.

_____

_____

_____

Listening

1. Find the verses that have the same meaning as the sentences below.

   a) You are going too fast and don't know what you want anymore.

   _____

   b) Why be scared if you know you're intelligent.

   _____

   c) I don't have enough time to do all that I have to do in a day.

   _____

   d) There's a right time for things to happen in your life.

   _____

2. Listen to the song and complete the verses.

   You've got your passion. _____
   But don't you know that only fools are satisfied?
   Dream on, but _____
   _____ *. Vienna waits for you!*

3. Do you agree with the stanza above? Talk to a partner about it.

After listening

1. Give a title to this stanza. Compare your answers with your friends.

   _____

Slow down, you crazy child.
Take the phone off the hook and disappear for a while.
It's all right you can afford to lose a day or two.
When will you realize? Vienna waits for you.

2. Read the sentence below and point out the contrasting discourse marker. Find other examples throughout the song.

Dream on, but don't imagine they'll all come true.

a) _____
b) _____
c) _____
d) _____

3. In pairs, summarize the meaning of the song in your own words.

_____
_____
_____
_____
_____

Atividades de música

Parte 2

Vinte atividades fotocopiáveis de 50 minutos

	Música	Cantor/ grupo	Tema	Gramática	Nível
1	"Wonderful tonight"	Eric Clapton	Love	Word order	Basic
2	"With my own two hands"	Ben Harper	World issues	Use of can Comparatives	Basic
3	"I believe I can fly"	R. Kelly	Self-esteem	Lexical and rhyming words	Basic
4	"Born this way"	Lady Gaga	Prejudice	Rhyming words and imperative	Basic
5	"A day in a life"	Beatles	Routine	Simple past	Basic
6	"I am not a girl, not yet a woman"	Britney Spears	Teenage fears	Opposing ideas	Basic
7	"Secrets"	One Republic	Secrets	Word order and lexical	Pre-intermediate
8	"Papa don't preach"	Madonna	Teenage pregnancy	Semantics, rhyming words and the use of should	Pre-intermediate
9	"Unwritten"	Natasha	Life and maturity	Use of the negative prefixes	Pre-intermediate
10	"Hallelujah"	Leonard Cohen	Religious concepts	Intonation and the use of *Used to*	Intermediate
11	"I dreamed a dream"	Les Misérables	Dreams	Use of the negative prefixes and simple past	Intermediate
12	"Smile"	Uncle Kracker	Happiness	Comparative and superlative, uses of *like*	Intermediate
13	"One"	U2	Relationships	Rhyming words	Intermediate
14	"Goodbye England's rose"	Elton John	Role models	Semantics	Intermediate
15	"The Only Exception"	Paramore	Divorce	Regular and irregular verbs in the past and use of the word *exception*	Intermediate
16	"Where is the love?"	The Black Eyed Peas	Political theme	Present continuous and rhyming words	Advanced
17	"Drops of Jupiter"	Train	Life after death	Use of the expression *Tell me*	Advanced
18	"Dear Mr. President"	Pink	Political views	Forming questions	Advanced
19	"If it was your last day"	Nickelback	Philosophical views of life	Giving advice, rhyming words and conditionals	Advanced
20	"Viva la vida"	Coldplay	Religious beliefs	Simple present and past	Advanced

Wonderful tonight

Eric Clapton

Disponível em: http://www.youtube.com/watch?v=vUSzL2leaFM

Acesso em: 24/07/2012

Before listening

1. Sit in pairs. Look at the columns below. Discuss the ideas with your partner and fill out the columns according to your beliefs.

What boys do before they go out to a party	What girls do before they go out to a party

Listening

1. Listen to the song. List the three things the girl does as she is getting ready to go out.

2. Listen again. What question does the girl in the song ask her partner? Think about three other questions girls ask their partners.

3. How does Eric Clapton describe the girl's hair? Look at the list below and put the words in the correct order.

blue / eyes / bright: _____

hair / black / short: _____

eyes / green / beautiful: _____

red / big / nose: _____

eye lashes / long / black: _____

4. Listen to the song while reading the lyrics and underline all the rhyming words. Check with a friend. Write them in the space provided and read them out loud.

_____

_____

_____

_____

_____

_____

_____

_____

_____

_____

After listening

1. Describe three friends using the correct word order. Write the description in the space provided.

_____

_____

_____

_____

_____

_____

_____

_____

_____

With my own two hands

Ben Harper

Disponível em: http://www.youtube.com/watch?v=_DBykcRxnPg

Acesso em: 24/07/2012 (Ben Harper)

Disponível em: http://www.youtube.com/watch?v=tdiZhJh5q3E

Acesso em: 24/07/2012 (Ben Harper e Jack Johnson)

Before listening

1. Read the title of the song and watch the first video clip (no sound). What do you think the song is about?

2. Watch the video clip again (with sound) and confirm your hypothesis.

3. Are you concerned about the world's problems? Do you think you can help as an individual?

_____

_____

_____

4. What can you do?

_____

_____

_____

Listening

1. Listen to the song sung by Ben Harper. Write five sentences he says you can do with your own two hands. Follow the example.

a) I can change the world.
b) I can _____
c) I _____
d) _____
e) _____
f) _____

2. There are four examples of comparatives in the lyrics of the song. Which are they?

a) _____
b) _____
c) _____
d) _____

After listening

1. Use the following adjectives to form sentences comparing places. Follow the example.

**clean – dirty – big – contaminated – small – large –
bad – important – peaceful – polluted**

a) São Paulo is bigger than Campinas.
b) _____
c) _____
d) _____
e) _____
f) _____
g) _____
h) _____
i) _____
j) _____

2. You have already listened to Ben Harper singing "With my own two hands" alone. Listen to the duet sung by Jack Johnson and Ben Harper and decide which one you like best. Use *"I prefer* _____
because _____ *."*

3. Talk to a partner. Agree to something you can both do for a week to help change the world.

I believe I can fly

R. Kelly

Disponível em: http://www.youtube.com/watch?v=16FdJrrAWSo

Acesso em: 24/07/2012

Before listening

1. Based on the title of the song, talk to a partner and predict: what will the lyrics of the song be about?

2. Watch the first two minutes of the video clip (with sound). Is it related to what you thought it might be? Justify.

Listening

1. Listen to the first stanza and order the verses.

( ) And life was nothing but an awful song
( ) I'm leaning on the everlasting arms
( ) If I can see it, then I can do it
( ) I used to think that I could not go on
( ) But now I know the meaning of true love
( ) If I just believe it, there's nothing to it

2. Listen to the song and complete the verses.

I believe I can fly
I believe I can touch the _____
I think about it every _____ *and* _____
Spread my wings and fly _____
I believe I can soar
I see me running through that _____ _____
I believe I can fly

3. What does he mean by "I believe I can fly"? Why does he feel like that at this moment?

   _____
   _____
   _____

4. Check True (T) or False (F). Justify using a verse from the song.

   ( ) Life was easy for him.
   ( ) He has found his love.
   ( ) He thinks life begins inside of him.
   ( ) He was having a nervous breakdown.

After listening

1. Watch the other two versions of the same song:

   Duet with Melanie Amaro: http://www.youtube.com/watch?v=o7oDz4omME4
   Glee cast: http://www.youtube.com/watch?v=qKPS1ueL_vE

   Which version do you like best? Why?

   _____
   _____
   _____
   _____
   _____

Born this way

Lady Gaga

Before listening

1. Based on the title of the song, talk to a partner and predict: what will the lyrics of the song be about?

2. Read these sentences taken from the song to confirm your hypothesis. Talk to your partner.

   You're black, white, beige, chola descent, you're Lebanese, you're orient...
   No matter gay, straight or bi, lesbian, transgendered life...
   I must be myself, respect my youth.
   Just love yourself.

3. Check the words related to what you agreed the song is about.

   ( ) prejudice
   ( ) bullying
   ( ) sexuality
   ( ) racism
   ( ) personality
   ( ) physical characteristics

Listening

1. a) Complete the sentences with the verbs below coherently.

    **hold – give – rejoice – don't be – listen – be –
    love – love – love – don't hide**

    So _____ your head up, girl and you'll go far, _____ to me when I say
    _____ _____ yourself in regret, just _____ yourself and you're set
    _____ _____ a drag, just _____ a queen
    _____ and _____ yourself today
    _____ yourself prudence and _____ your friends

    b) Listen to the song to check your work.

2. Listen to the song. Find the words that rhyme with:

    youth: _____
    far: _____
    way: _____
    regret: _____

After listening

1. Read the sentences above and answer these questions.

    a) What verb tense is being used?

    _____

    b) When do you use this verb tense?

    _____

2. Complete the sentences.

    a) To form the imperative affirmative we use the _____ of the verb.
    b) To form the imperative negative we use _____ + the _____
        of the verb.

3. Talk to a partner about prejudice and write two sentences using verbs in the imperative.

a) _____

b) _____

4. Read the stanzas below. Give each stanza a title.

I'm beautiful in my way
'Cause God makes no mistakes
I'm on the right track, baby
I was born this way

Don't hide yourself in regret
Just love yourself and you're set
I'm on the right track, baby
I was born this way

_____
_____
_____
_____

A day in the life

The Beatles

Disponível em: http://www.youtube.com/watch?v=P-Q9D4dcYng

Acesso em: 25/07/2012

Before listening

1. Think about a day in a life of a person in any part of the world. Can you describe an average person's routine? Use the present tense.

2. Are routines the same all over the world?

3. In your opinion what factors have a major influence and may make people's routines different. List at least five things that can differentiate one routine from another.

    _____

    _____

    _____

    _____

    _____

Listening

1. Listen to the song. List in the chart below the first ten verbs in the past tense.

2. Look at the verbs you listed in the chart. Write a paragraph using as many as you can telling us about something you did last week.

_____

_____

_____

_____

_____

3. Find the opposite meanings of the following words in the song:

sad: _____

laugh: _____

before: _____

love: _____

small: _____

late: _____

upstairs: _____

After listening

1. Tell a friend about a day in your life last week. Make sure you use the past tense.

2. Find a song that talks about a day in a life. Compare the lyrics. Do they have the same meaning?

I am not a girl, not yet a woman

Britney Spears

Disponível em: http://www.youtube.com/watch?v=IlV7RhT6zHs

Acesso em: 25/07/2012

Before listening

1. Read the sentences below. Do you agree or disagree? Check what you think. Talk to a partner.

   a) Many kids announce the beginning of adolescence with a change in behavior around their parents.
   b) At this age, teenagers become more distant and more independent from their parents.
   c) Having fears or anxieties about certain things can be helpful because it makes adolescents behave in a safe way.
   d) Teenagers' peers often become much more important, compared with their parents, in terms of taking decisions.

2. Answer these questions. Exchange ideas with a partner.

   a) If you are a teenager, what are your fears?
   b) If you are an adult, what were your fears when you were a teenager?

Listening

1. Listen to the first stanza. Order the verses.

    ( )   *But now I know*
    ( )   *Feels like I'm caught in the middle*
    ( )   *I used to think I had the answers to everything*
    ( )   *That life doesn't always go my way*
    ( )   *That's when I realize*
    ( )   *While I'm in between*
    ( )   *I'm not a girl, not yet a woman*
    ( )   *I'm not a girl*
    ( )   *All I need is time, a moment that is mine*

2. Fill in the blanks.

    There is no need to _____ *me*
    It's _____ *that I*
    Learn to face up to this on my _____
    I've seen so _____ _____ *than you know now*
    So don't _____ *me to shut my* _____

3. Find the opposite words in the lyrics. Write a paragragh using them.

    open: _____
    boy: _____
    questions: _____
    nothing: _____
    man: _____

    _____
    _____
    _____
    _____
    _____
    _____
    _____

After listening

1. Complete these sentences using your own ideas.

    a) I used to _____

    b) It feels like I _____

    c) Now I realize _____

    d) All I need is _____

    e) There is no need to _____

2. Write a small paragraph explaining what you understood about the lyrics. What is the main idea?

    _____

    _____

    _____

    _____

    _____

    _____

Secrets

One Republic

Disponível em: http://www.youtube.com/watch?v=qHm9MG9xw1o

Acesso em: 25/07/2012

Before listening

1. Answer these questions as a group.

   a) Define the word: secret.
   b) Do you have any secrets?
   c) If so, do you share your secrets with anyone?
   d) When people have secrets do you think it makes their lives easier or more difficult? Justify your answer.
   e) Do you think people are able to keep secrets?

Listening

1. Listen to the song and find the opposites to the following words:

   interesting: _____

   lies: _____

   put on: _____

   near: _____

   small: _____

   falls: _____

   high: _____

2. Read the chorus below. Look at the verbs below. Fill in the spaces according to what you feel is correct without listening to the song. Then correct it by listening.

_____ *me what you* _____ *to hear*
Something that'll _____ *those ears*
Sick of all the insincere
So I'm gonna _____ *all my secrets away*
This time
Don't _____ *another perfect lie*
Don't _____ *if critics never jumped in line*
I'm gonna give all my secrets away

care – want – tell – need – like – give

3. Check True (T) or False (F). Justify using a verse.

He thinks his life is boring.
(   ) _____
 He is not going to tell his secrets.
(   ) _____
He has a big family.
(   ) _____
He is tired of lying.
(   ) _____

4. Find in the song the verse where he describes a car. Write it below.

_____

After listening

1. Unscramble the sentences below using the correct word order:

a) eyes / he / has / blue / big

_____

b) my / long / has / hair / black / father

_____

c) small / my / has / a / car / friend / green

_____

d) dog / black / has / a / big / nose / my

_____

e) beautiful / the / has / many / pink / sky / clouds

_____

f) he / whiskers / has / cat / black / long

_____

g) the / wall / has / my / house / many / blue / stain / big / marks / on

_____

2. Do you think he was happy that he had secrets?

_____

3. Would you like to share a secret?

_____

Papa don't preach

Madonna

Disponível em: http://www.youtube.com/watch?v=RkxqxWgEEz4

Acesso em: 26/07/2012

Before listening

1. Do you know many teenage girls who got themselves pregnant?

2. Do you have a strong opinion about what a girl should do in this case? What about the boy? What should he do?

3. Can you think about another song that talks about this subject?

Listening

1. Listen to the song and check True (T) or False (F)

    ( )   She is angry at her father.
    ( )   She thinks her father is going to be upset.
    ( )   She wants her father's advice.
    ( )   She loves her boyfriend.
    ( )   Her boyfriend does not treat her nicely.
    ( )   Her friends tell her not to give up the baby.
    ( )   She does not want the baby.
    ( )   Her father taught her right from wrong.

2. Find a verse in the song with the same meaning as:

a) Dad, I am sure you are going to be disturbed.

_____

b) I know I am not experienced.

_____

c) I need someone to give me a recommendation.

_____

d) I have my mind set, I am having my baby.

_____

e) I need you strength now, dad.

_____

3. a) Fill out the missing words from this stanza.

He _____ that he's going to _____
We can raise a _____
Maybe we'll be _____
It's a _____

b) Which are the rhyming words?
The rhyming words are _____

After listening

1. Read the lyrics of the song. Find a word she uses that has the same meaning as *should*.

_____

2. Talk to a friend. List six things teenagers should and should not do related to this topic.

_____

Unwritten

Natasha Bedingfield

Disponível em: http://www.youtube.com/watch?v=cFFBSSntZgs

Acesso em: 26/07/2012 (British version)

Before listening

1. In your opinion, when does a person start leading his/her own life?

( )   when he/she is born.
( )   when he/she is 13 years old.
( )   when he/she starts university.
( )   when he/she gets married.
( )   when he/she starts living by himself.
( )   when he/she gets his/her first job.
( )   _____

2. Read this stanza. Check True (T) or False (F) according to what you understand.

I am unwritten, can't read my mind, I'm undefined
I'm just beginning, the pen's in my hand, ending unplanned
Staring at the blank page before you
Open up the dirty window
Let the sun illuminate the words that you could not find

( )   I'm writing a book.
( )   I'm taking the first steps in my life.
( )   I'm confused.
( )   I feel empty.

3. Read this second stanza and give it a title.

   _____

   "Release your inhibition, feel the rain on your skin
   No one else can feel it for you, only you can let it in
   No one else, no one else can speak the words on your lips"

4. Read the lines below, talk to a partner and write a sentence explaining their meaning.

   I break tradition, sometimes my tries, are outside the lines
   We've been conditioned to not make mistakes, but I can't live that way.

   _____

   _____

5. Watch the video clip (no sound). Does it have any connection to the lyrics of the song? Describe some scenes of the video.

   _____

   _____

Listening

1. Watch the video again (with sound). What other meanings can you add to the song?

   _____

   _____

   _____

   _____

   _____

2. Listen to the song and write words with the prefix *un-*. Follow the example.

*un*written

_____

_____

_____

3. What does the prefix *un-* mean?

_____

After listening

1. Use the following negative prefixes to form new words.

	un-	dis-	i-
important			
relevant			
able			
successful			
honest			
logical			
order			

2. Choose two words from the chart above. Write sentences with them.

_____

_____

Hallelujah

Leonard Cohen

Disponível em: http://www.youtube.com/watch?v=YrLk4vdY28Q

Acesso em: 26/07/2012

Before listening

1. Look at the title of the song. What meanings can you give to this word?

2. Listen to the song for gist. What do you think it is about?

3. Look at the words below. Write down the opposites. Check with a partner.

weak: _____

fix: _____

after: _____

together: _____

hot: _____

fixed: _____

above: _____

hate: _____

day: _____

worst: _____

everything: _____

dark: _____

Listening

1. Listen to the song and find the words you wrote in the previous activity.

2. Listen again. Pay attention to the intonation given after each Hallelujah sang in each verse: happy, sad, with faith, desperate, cold, broken, excited... Discuss with a friend.

3. Read this verse. Listen and order it.

    ( )   *Love is not a victory march*
    ( )   *Baby I have been here before*
    ( )   *I used to live alone before I knew you.*
    ( )   *It's a cold and it's a broken Hallelujah*
    ( )   *I know this room, I've walked this floor*
    ( )   *I've seen your flag on the marble arch*

After listening

1. Look at the expression: "I used to live alone before I knew you". Talk to a partner and tell him/her things you used to do but don't do anymore.

2. Listen to the song again. What do you think it is about? Is your interpretation the same as in question 2 of the listening activity?

I dreamed a dream

Les Misérables

Disponível em: http://www.youtube.com/watch?v=3uFww9a3D4E

Acesso em: 25/07/2012

Before listening

Talk to a partner about the following.

1. How would your life be in your dreams? Where would you live? What would you do? Who would you live with?

2. Write down five words that come to your mind when thinking about dreams. What would make your dreams come true?

    _____

    _____

    _____

    _____

    _____

3. Compare your notes with other friends and see if you have similar dreams.

Listening

1. Complete the sentences below with the words you think fit best.

   a) Her hopes were _____ .
   b) Life was worth _____ .
   c) Love would never _____ .
   d) God was _____ .
   e) She was _____ and not _____ .
   f) All songs were not _____ .
   g) All wine was not _____ .

2. Listen to the first stanza and complete the sentences below according to the song.

   a) Her hopes were _____ .
   b) Life was worth _____ .
   c) Love would never _____ .
   d) God was _____ .
   e) She was _____ and not _____ .
   f) All songs were not _____ .
   g) All wine was not _____ .

3. a) Is she hopeful in this stanza? List five words or sentences that indicate her hope.

   _____
   _____
   _____
   _____
   _____

   b) Listen to the stanza again. Fill out the chart using the negative prefix used in the song.

afraid	
sung	
tasted	

c) Fill out the chart using the prefixes below:

mis – il – un – re – im – dis

lucky	
behave	
view	
obey	
healthy	
happy	
possible	
honest	
legal	
connect	
cover	
sense	

3. Listen to the second stanza. Is she hopeful? Write down the words or sentences that indicate her state of mind.

_____

_____

_____

_____

4. Listen to the whole song. Which verb tense predominates in the song?

_____

5. Read the lyrics and underline the verb tense you stated in activity 5.

6. Listen to the last stanza. Did her dreams come true? What line states that?

_____

_____

After listening

1. Play a game following your teacher's instructions.

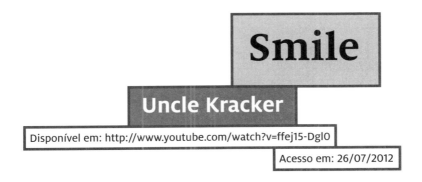

Disponível em: http://www.youtube.com/watch?v=ffej15-Dgl0

Acesso em: 26/07/2012

Before listening

1. What makes you smile? List five things.

2. Read this quote. Talk to a partner and explain it in your own words.

   "Sometimes your joy is the source of your smile, but sometimes your smile can be the source of your joy." *Thich Nhat Hanh*

3. Think of someone you know who is always smiling. Do you think they are happier people?

Listening

1. Listen to the first stanza. Write the comparative and superlative words you find in the chart below.

COMPARATIVE	SUPERLATIVE

2. Make sentences using the words you found.

_____
_____
_____
_____
_____
_____

3. Look at the sentences below. Complete them with any word you think is appropriate.

a) Smile like _____
b) You make me sing like a _____
c) You make me dance like a _____
d) You make me shine like a _____
e) You make me feel like a _____
f) I look like a _____

4. Listen to the song and compare what you wrote to the song. Complete the gaps.

You make me smile like the _____
Fall out of bed, sing like _____
Dizzy in my head, spin like a _____
Crazy on a Sunday night
You make me dance like a _____
Forget how to breathe
Shine like _____ *, buzz like a* _____
Just the thought of you can drive me wild
Ohh, you make me smile

After listening

1. Can you think of a person who always makes you smile? Talk to a friend about this person.

2. Look at the list of words below. Write down a sentence using the superlative form and the comparative. Exchange your sentences with a partner.

good – happy – big – cool – fun – funny – boring – beautiful – interesting

a) _____

b) _____

c) _____

d) _____

e) _____

f) _____

g) _____

h) _____

i) _____

3. Look below at the different uses of the word "like":

- *What's he/she like?* — 'What ... like?'. It is used to ask about a person's personality.
- *What does he like?* — It is used to talk about preferences. It is usually followed by the 'ing' form of the verb. Ex: *I like travelling abroad.*
- *What does she look like?* — 'Like' is used as a preposition to express physical appearance. 'Like' can also mean 'similar to', like in the song.
- *What would you like to drink?* — It is used to express wishes. Ex: *I would like to drink a glass of water.*

Answer the following questions:

a) What would you like to drink?

_____

b) What does your brother/sister/cousin look like?

_____

c) What does your mother like to do?

_____

d) What is your Math teacher like?

_____

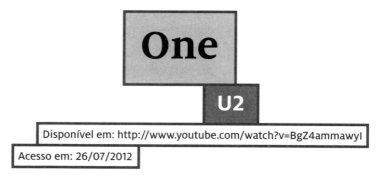

Disponível em: http://www.youtube.com/watch?v=BgZ4ammawyI

Acesso em: 26/07/2012

Before listening

1. In pairs, answer these questions:

    a) Do you think relationships are easy?
    b) List different types of relationships.
    c) Just because two people are together do you think they should have the same opinion?
    d) Can you love a person who is completely different than yourself?
    e) Are we all influenced by society's rules?
    f) Are we meant to think the same? Does society impose that?

2. a) Look up the word "blame" in the dictionary. Write it below.

    _____

    _____

    _____

    _____

    b) When a relationship ends who do we normally blame: ourselves or other people?

    _____

    _____

    _____

    _____

Listening

1. Listen to the first three stanzas. Number the sentences below according to the meaning of each stanza.

   a) ( ) You need to look after your love or else it will leave you.
   b) ( ) Now you have someone to blame, do you feel better?
   c) ( ) As nobody gave you love, you think I should not have it.

2. In the fourth stanza he says:

   We're one, but we're not the same
   We get to carry each other, carry each other

   a) Talk to a friend and interpret these two verses. Share your answers with the rest of the group. Take into consideration the questions answered in the *Before Listening* activity.

3. a) Listen and order these two stanzas.

   ( ) *You ask me to enter, but then you make me crawl*
   ( ) *You say:*
   ( ) *We get to carry each other, carry each other.*
   ( ) *Love is a temple, love a higher law*
   ( ) *One life, but we're not the same.*
   ( ) *And I can't keep holding on to what you got*
   ( ) *One love, one blood*
   ( ) *Love is a temple, love the higher law*
   ( ) *One life you got to do what you should.*
   ( ) *When all you got is hurt.*
   ( ) *One life with each other: sisters, brothers.*
   ( ) *One! One!*

   b) When reading the first verses of the stanzas above do you think these people will stay together? What verse shows that?

   _____
   _____
   _____

c) Do you think this song is a love song? If not, what else can he be talking about?

_____

_____

_____

_____

d) Listen to the whole song and find the rhyming words.

_____

_____

_____

_____

After listening

1. Sit in pairs. When the teacher says "go", list all the famous couples you know in two minutes. The pair that lists the most wins.

2. Can you think of a famous perfect couple?

_____

_____

_____

_____

Goodbye England's rose

Elton John

Disponível em: http://www.youtube.com/watch?v=VtHS2xBRUmI&feature=related

Acesso em: 26/07/2012

Before listening

Discuss with a friend.

1. Look at the title of the song. Do you know who this song is a tribute to?

2. Discuss in pairs what you know about this person. What happened to her and why was this song written for her?

3. Think about other songs that were written as a tribute to someone. Exchange ideas with your friends.

4. What kinds of words would you expect to have in a song as a tribute to someone? Write down five words and compare your answers.

_____

_____

_____

_____

_____

Listening

1. Listen to the song and complete the sentences:

    The lives were _____ _____

    You belong to _____ _____ .

    The stars _____ _____ *your name*

    Like a candle _____ _____ .

    These empty days _____ _____ _____

    Truth brings us _____ _____ .

    _____ *you brought us through the* _____ .

    From a country lost _____ _____ _____ .

2. Read the stanzas. Match the following titles to each stanza according to the context. Justify your answer. Correct the previous activity using the stanzas below.

    a) You were a compassionate person.
    b) You will never be forgotten.
    c) You helped people and gave them hope.
    d) You made us happy with your smile.

    ( )
    Goodbye England's rose
    May you ever grow in our hearts
    You were the grace that placed itself
    Where lives were torn apart
    You called out to our country
    And you whispered to those in pain
    Now you belong to heaven
    And the stars spell out your name

    ( )
    And it seems to me you lived your life
    Like a candle in the wind
    Never fading with the sunset
    When the rain set in

And your footsteps will always fall here
Along England's greenest hills
Your candle's burned out long before
Your legend ever will

( )
Loveliness we've lost
These empty days without your smile
This torch we'll always carry
For our nation's golden child
And even though we try
The truth brings us to tears
All our words cannot express
The joy you brought us through the years

( )
Goodbye England's rose
May you ever grow in our hearts
You were the grace that placed itself
Where lives were torn apart
Goodbye England's rose
From a country lost without your soul
Who'll miss the wings of your compassion
More than you'll ever know

After listening

1. What do you think the expression "candle in the wind" means in this stanza? Explain the stanza in your own words.

   And it seems to me you lived your life
   Like a candle in the wind
   Never fading with the sunset
   When the rain set in
   And your footsteps will always fall here

Along England's greenest hills
Your candle's burned out long before
Your legend ever will

2. If you could write a song for someone, who would it be for? What would you write about?

_____

_____

_____

_____

The only exception

Paramore

Disponível em: http://www.youtube.com/watch?v=-J7J_IWUhls

Acesso em: 26/07/2012

Before listening

Discuss the following questions in pairs.

1. Do you know many divorced couples?

2. Why do you think divorce rates are so high today?

3. List countries that have a different concept towards marriage. Explain the concepts.

4. What is your belief about marriage?

5. Do you believe in soul mates?

Listening

1. Listen to the first stanza. What happened to her father?

2. Listen to the second stanza. What did her mother say?

3. Listen to the second stanza again. How did the parents' relationship influence the singer?

4. Listen to the whole song. List the verbs you hear in the past in the correct column.

Regular verbs in the past	Irregular verbs in the past

5. In what stanza does the singer say that she is happy to be alone?

6. Order the following verses.

( ) *I know you're leaving*
( ) *Leave me with some kind of proof it's not a dream*
( ) *But I can't*
( ) *Let go of what's in front of me here*
( ) *In the morning, when you wake up*
( ) *I've got a tight grip on reality*

7. Is this stanza positive or negative? Why?

8. Read the lyrics of the song. Can you find a verse that has a positive meaning and comforts the singer?

After listening

1. Do you believe there are exceptions for everything? Can you think of something that was an exception to the rule in your life?

2. Read the sentences below. Write three more sentences using the word exception.

I like to eat vegetables, with one exception of Brussels sprouts.
I will not take any essays after the deadline. I will make no exceptions.

Where is the love?

The Black Eyed Peas

Disponível em: http://www.youtube.com/watch?v=WpYeekQkAdc&ob=av2n

Acesso em: 27/07/2012

Before listening

1. Watch the video clip with no sound. Write down five words that come to your mind while watching the video. What do you think this song is about?

   _____

   _____

2. Look at the stanza below. Undeline the verbs in present continuous tenses and the two words that rhyme. Explain the stanza in your own words to a partner.

   People killing, people dying
   Children hurt and you hear them crying
   Can you practice what you preach?
   And would you turn the other cheek?

3. Sit in pairs. Read the stanza below and answer the following questions:

   a) Do you think children are influenced by the media? Give examples.

   b) What are the rhyming words in this stanza:

      Wrong information always shown by the media
      Negative images is the main criteria
      Infecting the young minds faster than bacteria

Kids wanna act like what they see in the cinema

Listening

1. Listen to the lyrics of the song. Write down five positives words and five negative words. Is the song more optimistic or pessimistic?

   _____

   _____

   _____

   _____

2. Listen to the song without looking at the lyrics. Clap your hands when you hear the following words:

   **meditate – attracted – living – discriminate –
   terrorism – preach – money – humanity**

3. Using as many words from above, make a sentence expressing your feelings.

   _____

   _____

   _____

   _____

4. Listen to the song and sing along.

After listening

1. Choose a stanza from the song. Classify it whether it is optimistic or pessimistic. Rewrite it in your own words.

   _____

   _____

   _____

   _____

   _____

   _____

   _____

Drops of Jupiter

Train

Disponível em: http://www.youtube.com/watch?v=7Xf-Lesrkuc

Acesso em: 27/07/2012

Before listening

1. Do you believe in life after death?

2. How do people deal with the loss of a loved one?

3. Do you believe you can grow and mature after the death of a loved one?

Listening

1. Patrick Monahan wrote this song for his mum. Listen to the song. Write down all the words you hear related to Space or seasons below. Check with your friends.

_____

_____

_____

_____

_____

_____

2. Why do you think he uses words related to the Space?

    _____
    _____
    _____
    _____
    _____

3. Look at the sentences below. Complete them as you wish, making sure they are coherent.

    Now that she's back _____
    Tracing her way _____
    She checks out _____
    Reminds me _____
    Now that she's back _____
    I'm afraid that _____
    Plain old Jane _____
    Who was too afraid to _____

4. Listen to the third stanza and match the sentences below.

    a) Now that she's back   ( ) through the constellation
    b) Tracing her way   ( ) in the atmosphere
    c) She checks out   ( ) told a story about a man
    d) Reminds me   ( ) Mozart while she does tae-bo
    e) Now that she's back   ( ) she might think of me as
    f) I'm afraid that   ( ) fly so he never did land
    g) Plain old Jane   ( ) from that soul vacation
    h) Who was too afraid to   ( ) that there's room to grow

5. Listen to the song and pay attention to all the sentences he uses after "tell me". Write them down. The first one is done for you.

    Tell me <u>did you sail across the sun?</u>
    Tell me _____
    Tell me _____
    Tell me _____
    Tell me _____

After listening

1. Talk to a friend. Choose a topic and use the expression "tell me" and maintain a conversation about the topic.

2. Can you think of other songs that talk about this topic? Report to the class.

Dear Mr. President

Pink

Disponível em: http://www.youtube.com/watch?v=32I6nk8hBGE

Acesso em: 27/07/2012

Before listening

1. Research on the Internet. Write a list of things that are the President's role as chief of state.

   _____

   _____

2. In your opinion do you think our president is fulfilling his/her role?

3. If you were president of Brazil which would be your first actions?

Listening

1. Listen to the second and third stanzas. What questions does Pink ask the President? List six.

   a) _____
   b) _____
   c) _____
   d) _____
   e) _____
   f) _____

2. Listen to the song and check True (T) or False (F)

   a) Pink asks the President:

   ( ) if he is proud.
   ( ) if he is lonely.
   ( ) If he has a wife.
   ( ) how he can take his daughter's rights away.

3. Check the things Pink defines as hard work.

   ( ) Minimum wage with a baby on the way.
   ( ) Working all day.
   ( ) Rebuilding your house after the bombs took them away.
   ( ) Working with your gay daughter.
   ( ) Building a bed out of a cardboard box.
   ( ) Working selling cocaine.

After listening

1. Talk to a friend. Write down the name of the President of the following countries. If you don't know, research on the net.

   France: _____
   Italy: _____
   United States: _____
   Argentina: _____
   Germany: _____

2. Discuss with a colleague what you would ask the President if you had an interview with him.

3. Research on the net the President that served the shortest term in office and the one that served the longest term in office in Brazil and in the United States.

   _____
   _____

If today was your last day

Nickelback

Disponível em: http://www.youtube.com/watch?v=lrXIQQ8PeRs

Acesso em: 25/07/2012

Before listening

Discuss in pairs:

1. Are you satisfied with the life you are living?

2. What would you do differently if you could change the past?

3. If you could control the future, what would you like your future to be like?

4. What would you do if you knew that today would be your last day on Earth?

5. Check the sentences you agree with and discuss them with a friend.

( ) Our days are gifts and not given rights
( ) What's worth the price is always worth the fight
( ) Every second counts 'cause there's no second try
( ) Live like you're never living twice

Listening

1. Listen to the first stanza. Write down three advice he was given. Check with a friend.

   a) _____

   b) _____

   c) _____

2. Listen to the third stanza and order the verses.

   ( )   *So live like you're never living twice*

   ( )   *Against the grain should be a way of life*

   ( )   *Every second counts 'cause there's no second try*

   ( )   *What's worth the price is always worth the fight*

   ( )   *Don't take the free ride in your own life*

3. Read the third stanza again. Discuss the meaning with your friends. Do you agree with the composer?

4. Listen to the whole song. Write the questions that begin with *would*.

   _____

   _____

   _____

   _____

   _____

   _____

   _____

   _____

   _____

   _____

5. Listen to this stanza and fill in the missing words. Fill in the chart with the words that rhyme.

   And would you call those _____ you never _____ ?

   Reminisce old _____ ?

   Would you _____ your _____ ?

   And would you find that one you're _____ of?

_____ *up and down to God above*

That you'd finally _____ *if today was your last day?*

see	of

After listening

1. Answer the questions below in pairs.

    What would you do if you had a million dollars?
    Who would you be if you could choose someone for a day?
    What would you do if today was your last day?
    What would you do if you won the lottery?
    Who would you like to meet if you could choose any celebrity?
    What would you do if you had the power to read people's mind?
    What would you say if the whole world was listening?
    If you had one wish, what would you wish for?
    If you could relive any moment in your life which moment would it be and why?

Viva la vida

Coldplay

Disponível em: http://www.youtube.com/watch?v=KTSG5PGCceM

Acesso em: 27/07/2012

Before listening

1. Ask a partner the following questions.

    a) Were you brought up in a religious family? Was religion an important part of your life when you were a child?
    b) How about today?
    c) Do you believe in Heaven and Hell?
    d) Do you believe you can be punished after death according to your actions?

2. Watch the clip (no sound). What musical instruments are played by the band?

Listening

1. Listen to the song and complete the verses.

    _____ *I held the key*
    _____ *the walls were closed on me*
    And I discovered that my castles _____
    Upon pillars of salt and pillars of _____ .

2. Listen to the song again and order these verses.

    ( ) *I know Saint Peter won't call my name*
    ( ) *But that was when I ruled the world*
    ( ) *For some reason I can't explain*
    ( ) *Never an honest word*

3. What do they mean?

    _____
    _____
    _____
    _____

4. Match the titles below to the stanzas you think they belong. There are three titles. Choose three stanzas.

    I built my power on unstable floor.
    I had the power but now there is no one by my side.
    People always want the king's head.

5. Listen to the song one more time. There are some religious references in the lyrics of "Viva la Vida". What are they? What do they refer to?

    _____
    _____
    _____
    _____

After listening

1. Read the verses below. Complete the chart classifying the verses that refer to the past and to the present. Follow the example.

    I used to rule the world
    Seas would rise when I gave the word
    Now in the morning I sleep alone
    Sweep the streets I used to own

I used to roll the dice
Feel the fear in my enemy's eyes
Listened as the crowd would sing
"Now the old king is dead! Long live the king!

PAST	PRESENT
I used to rule the world.	Now I sleep alone.

2. How can you interpret these verses?

_____

_____

_____

_____

_____

_____

Informações técnicas, *Teaching tips, Answer keys e Lyrics*

Parte 1

Vinte atividades fotocopiáveis de 20 minutos

Everything

Michael Bublé

INFORMAÇÕES TÉCNICAS

Composição: Michael Bublé e Alan Chang
Estilo: Pop
Cantor: Michael Bublé
Site oficial: http://www.michaelbuble.com
Tema: Amor

Informações sobre o autor e a música

Michael Bublé é cantor, ator e compositor canadense. Ele ganhou vários prêmios, incluindo três Grammy e vários Juno Awards.

Teaching tips

Essa é uma atividade curta (15 minutos) para ser usada no início ou no final da aula. Durante o *Before listening* peça aos alunos que tentem completar os versos levando em consideração o contexto e a rima. Os alunos devem comparar suas respostas com um colega. Em seguida, ouçam a música para verificar as respostas. Coloque a música novamente e peça que o alunos retirem palavras ou expressões positivas. Peça que completem o quadro com essas expressões e, em pares, pensem em palavras com conotação negativa relacionadas a essas palavras/expressões. Durante o *After listening*, organize a classe em pares e peça que escrevam as sentenças. Em seguida, os alunos fazem a atividade de vocabulário relacionando as expressões com seus correspondentes em português de acordo com o contexto.

Answer key

Before listening

You're a falling star, you're the getaway <u>car</u>.
You're the line in the sand when I go too <u>far</u>.
You're the swimming pool, on an August <u>day</u>
And you're the perfect thing to <u>say</u>.
And you play it coy but it's kind of cute.
Ah, when you smile at me you know exactly what you <u>do</u>
Baby, don't pretend that you don't know it's <u>true</u>
'cause you can see it when I look at <u>you</u>.
You're a <u>carousel</u>, you're a wishing <u>star</u>,
And you light me up, when you ring my <u>bells</u>.
You're a mystery, you're from outer space,
You're every minute of my everyday.

Listening

1. Listen to the song and check your work.

2.

POSITIVE	NEGATIVE
Perfect	Imperfect
Smile	Cry
Cute	Ugly
True	False
Don't pretend	Pretend
Make me sing	Make me cry
Love	Hate
Everything	nothing

After listening

1. Open Answer.

2. (f) poço dos desejos — a wishing well
   (a) estrela cadente — a falling star
   (b) carro em fuga — the getaway car
   (e) você me faz lembrar — you ring my bell
   (c) fazer-se de boba — play it coy
   (d) engraçadinha — kind of cute
   (h) Espaço sideral — outer space
   (g) não finja — don't pretend

Lyrics

"Everything"

You're a falling star, you're the getaway car
You're the line in the sand when I go too far
You're the swimming pool, on an August day
And you're the perfect thing to say

And you play it coy but it's kind of cute
Ah, when you smile at me you know exactly what you do
Baby, don't pretend that you don't know it's true
'cause you can see it when I look at you

Chorus
And in this crazy life, and through these crazy times
It's you, it's you, you make me sing.
You're every line, you're every word, you're everything.

You're a carousel, you're a wishing well,
And you light me up, when you ring my bell.
You're a mystery, you're from outer space,
You're every minute of my everyday.

And I can't believe, that I'm your man,
And I get to kiss you baby just because I can.
Whatever comes our way, ah we'll see it through,
And you know that's what our love can do.

Chorus

So, la, la, la, la, la, la, la
So, la, la, la, la, la, la, la

Chorus
And in this crazy life, and through these crazy times
It's you, it's you, you make me sing.
You're every line, you're every word, you're everything.
You're every song, and I sing along.
'Cause you're my everything.
Yeah, yeah

So, la, la, la, la, la, la, la
So, la, la, la, la, la, la, la

Imagine

John Lennon

INFORMAÇÕES TÉCNICAS

Composição: John Lennon
Estilo: Pop rock
Cantor: John Lennon
Site: http://www.johnlennon.com
Tema: Paz, guerra, governo, pobreza

Informações sobre o cantor e a música

John Winston Lennon, nascido em Liverpool, em 1940, foi um dos fundadores do grupo The Beatles. John Lennon formou ao lado de Paul McCartney uma das duplas de compositores mais famosas de todos os tempos. Foi assassinado em 1980 em Nova York. Essa música foi escrita durante a guerra do Vietnã, no governo Nixon. Lennon nos leva a imaginar a vida sem governos, religiões, guerras, posses... ou seja, a paz completa.

Teaching tips

Pergunte aos seus alunos o que eles conhecem sobre John Lennon. Organize-os em pares e peça-lhes que escrevam sobre o que seria um mundo perfeito para eles. Em seguida, as duplas podem compartilhar as ideias. Você pode colocar as sugestões na lousa. Peça aos alunos que ouçam a música toda e completem as sentenças com base nas ideias de mundo perfeito de Lennon e em seguida verifiquem as respostas com um colega. Na questão 2 do *Listening*, os alunos ouvem a música novamente e encontram dois pares de rimas. No *After listening*, os alunos deverão escrever uma sentença com suas impressões sobre a música e postar na sua rede social favorita. Em seguida eles deverão ouvir a música novamente, encontrar os antônimos e escrever uma sentença com eles. No final, os alunos podem cantar assistindo ao clipe.

Answer key

Before listening

1. Open answers. Suggestions:

    a) In my world there is happiness, food for everybody, peace, clean water, nice weather.
    b) In my world there are good people, honest politicians, animals, flowers.
    c) In my world there is no hunger, no war, no pollution, no prejudice.
    d) In my world there are no natural disasters (floods, tornadoes, hurricanes, volcanic eruptions, earthquakes, tsunamis).

Listening

1. a) There's <u>only sky, peace and brotherhood.</u>
    b) There's no <u>heaven, no hell, no religion, no greed, no hunger, no possessions</u>.

2. Try / sky
    Do / too
    Can / Man

After listening

1. Suggestion:
    I think "Imagine" by John Lennon is a wonderful song because it's about peace and brotherhood.

2. Below / above
    Easy / hard
    Live / die
    War / peace
    Generosity / greed

3. Sing together.

Lyrics

"Imagine"

Imagine there's no Heaven
It's easy if you try
No hell below us
Above us only sky
Imagine all the people
Living for today.
Imagine there's no countries
It isn't hard to do
Nothing to kill or die for
And no religion too
Imagine all the people
Living life in peace.
You may say that I'm a dreamer
But I'm not the only one
I hope someday you'll join us
And the world will be as one.
Imagine no possessions
I wonder if you can
No need for greed or hunger
A brotherhood of man
Imagine all the people
Sharing all the world.
You may say I'm a dreamer
But I'm not the only one
I hope someday you'll join us
And the world will live as one.

You've got a friend in me

Randy Newman

INFORMAÇÕES TÉCNICAS

Composição: Randy Newman
Estilo: Pop rock
Cantora: Randy Newman
Site oficial: www.randynewman.com
Tema: amizade

Informações sobre o autor e a música

"You've got a friend in me" foi escrita e cantada por Randy Newman, além de ser tema musical dos filmes *Toy story* 1, 2 e 3 (1995, 1999 e 2010). Ela é tocada no início do filme *Toy story* 3, estabelecendo a importância de Woody para Andy.

Teaching tips

Esta é uma atividade curta (15 minutos) que pode ser feita no início ou no final da aula. Inicie organizando a classe em pares e pedindo que leiam as palavras do quadro e respondam à pergunta. Mostre o vídeo sem som e pergunte qual é o seu tema. Peça aos alunos que conversem em grupos de quatro. Em seguida, os alunos respondem individualmente as perguntas do exercício 3 e trocam informações com seus pares. Os alunos ouvem a música e ordenam as estrofes. Peça-lhes que verifiquem as respostas com os colegas. O último exercício pode ser feito em casa.

Answer key

Before listening

1. Open answer. Suggestion:
   They remind me of my friends, my parents, brothers and sisters, husband/wife.

2. It's about a boy and his favorite toy.

3. Open answers.

Listening

1. (5) (2) (1) (4) (3)

2. Bigger, smarter, stronger.

After listening

Fraternity
Respect
Individual
Empathy
New
Donate

Lyrics

"You've got a friend in me"

You've got a friend in me
You've got a friend in me
When the road looks rough ahead
And you're miles and miles
From your nice warm bed
Just remember what your old pal said
You've got a friend in me
You've got a friend in me
You've got a friend in me
You've got a friend in me
You've got troubles, well I've got 'me too
There isn't anything I wouldn't do for you
We stick together and we see it through
You've got a friend in me
You've got a friend in me
Some other folks might be
A little bit smarter than I am
Bigger and stronger too
Maybe
But none of them will ever love you the way I do
It's me and you
And as the years go by
our friendship will never die
You're gonna see
It's our destiny
You've got a friend in me
You've got a friend in me

Ebony and ivory

Paul McCartney e Stevie Wonder

INFORMAÇÕES TÉCNICAS

Composição: Paul McCartney
Estilo: Pop
Cantores: Paul McCartney e Stevie Wonder
Site oficial: http://www.paulmccartney.com
Tema: integração e harmonia racial, racismo, preconceito

Informações sobre os cantores e a música

Essa música faz parte do álbum *McCartney Tug of war*. Foi escrita por Paul McCartney e gravada por ele e Stevie Wonder, embora essa gravação tenha sido feita em estúdio separadamente em 1982. Após 28 anos, Paul e Stevie se apresentaram ao vivo, na Casa Branca, para uma plateia na qual estava presente o presidente Obama.

Teaching tips

Organize a classe em pares. Para o *Before listening* escreva o título da música e o primeiro verso na lousa e peça aos alunos que deduzam o que as palavras significam, a que fazem referência e sobre o que será a letra da música de Paul McCartney. Chame a atenção dos alunos para o fato de Paul McCartney fazer dueto com Stevie Wonder. Pergunte onde o racismo e o preconceito estão mais evidentes no mundo de hoje. Peça que preencham o quadro.

Dependendo do nível de seus alunos, essas atividades podem ser feitas na língua materna, pois têm como objetivo a contextualização. No *Listening*, os alunos ouvem a primeira estrofe e retiram os verbos que estão no presente. Para fazer a segunda atividade os alunos ouvem novamente e procuram as palavras que rimam com as palavras dadas. Ao ouvir mais uma vez os alunos buscam palavras antônimas. No *After listening* os alunos escolhem quatro verbos da primeira atividade e escrevem sentenças no tempo presente. É uma oportunidade para rever a forma afirmativa, negativa e interrogativa do presente e a terceira pessoa.

Answer key

Before listening

1. Open answer.
   Suggestion:
   They are about racism, prejudice and racial integration.

2. They refer to the materials ebony (ébano) and ivory (marfim) used in a piano keyboard. They also refer to Afro American and white people.

3. Open answers.

RACISM/PREJUDICE	RACIAL INTEGRATION
Africa	Brazil
Middle East	England
India	The United States
Afghanistan	Canada, Australia

4. Open answer

Listening

1. live, know, are, go, there is, learn, need. Present tense.

2. harmony: ebony, ivory
   keyboard: Lord
   live: give
   know: go

3. bad: good
   dead: <u>alive</u>
   take: <u>give</u>
   none: <u>everyone</u>
   apart: <u>together</u>
   nowhere: <u>everywhere</u>

After listening

Open answers.

Lyrics

"Ebony and ivory"

Ebony and ivory live together in perfect harmony
Side by side on my piano keyboard, oh lord, why don't we?
We all know that people are the same wherever we go
There is good and bad in everyone,
We learn to live, we learn to give
Each other what we need to survive together alive.

Ebony and ivory live together in perfect harmony
Side by side on my piano keyboard, oh lord why don't we?

Ebony, ivory living in perfect harmony
Ebony, ivory, ooh

We all know that people are the same wherever we go
There is good and bad in everyone
We learn to live, we learn to give
Each other what we need to survive together alive.

Ebony and ivory live together in perfect harmony
Side by side on my piano keyboard, oh lord why don't we?

Ebony, ivory living in perfect harmony

Somewhere only we know

Keane

INFORMAÇÕES TÉCNICAS

Composição: Keane
Estilo: Pop rock
Integrantes: Tim Rice-Oxley, compositor e pianista;
Tom Chaplin, vocalista; Richard Hughes, bateria
Site oficial: www.keanemusic.com
Tema: diverso

Informações sobre o autor e a música

A música "Somewhere only we know" é cantada pelo grupo inglês de rock alternativo Keane. É o primeiro single do álbum Hopes and Fears e foi um hit internacional no ano de 2004. Eles citam muitas influências, incluindo The Beatles, The Ramones, U2, Depeche Mode, A-Ha, Oasis, R.E.M., The Smiths, Radiohead, Queen, Pet Shop Boys e Paul Simon. Strangeland é o trabalho mais recente da banda.

Teaching tips

Peça aos alunos que leiam o título da música e pergunte-lhes se eles têm um lugar secreto, que somente uma pessoa conhece. Faça a primeira atividade do *Before listening* com eles. Eles devem ler as atividades do *Listening* para depois ouvir a música com um objetivo claro. Na primeira atividade eles devem anotar todos os verbos da primeira e segunda estrofe que estão no passado. Em seguida devem achar todas as palavras que rimam nessas mesmas estrofes. Na terceira tarefa eles devem descrever o local.

Na questão seguinte leia em voz alta todas as palavras. Peça aos alunos que ouçam a música novamente e que procurem palavras que rimam com as que você leu. Se houver tempo peça aos alunos que façam a mesma coisa: um aluno escolhe uma palavra que rima com algum palavra que está na música. Ele diz em voz alta para a classe. Os outros alunos devem encontrar na música alguma palavra que rime com a palavra dita.

Na tarefa de *After listening* eles devem completar o quadro e usar as palavras de forma adequada formando sentenças. Essa atividade pode ser oral. Cada aluno pode dizer uma frase usando uma das palavras. Verifique se eles entendem a diferença.

Answer key

Before listening

1.   Open answer.

2.   Open answer.

3.   a)   shopping malls, movies, parks, theatres etc.
     b)   quiet restaurants, calm places, walk in the woods etc.
     c)   movies, shopping malls, theatres.
     d)   restaurants, meeting rooms.

Listening

1.   a)   walked, knew, felt, sat.
     b)   land / hand; feet / complete; gone / on; in / begin
     c)   He is in a forest, near a river.

2.   a)   meat: feet, complete
     b)   case: place
     b)   mend: end
     b)   worth: earth

After listening

1.

somewhere	everywhere	anywhere
someone	everyone	anyone
sometime	everytime	anytime
something	everything	anything

2. Open answer.

Lyrics

"Somewhere only we know"

I walked across an empty land
I knew the pathway like the back of my hand
I felt the earth beneath my feet
Sat by the river and it made me complete

Oh! Simple thing where have you gone
I'm getting old and I need something to rely on
So tell me when you're gonna let me in
I'm getting tired and I need somewhere to begin

I came across a fallen tree
I felt the branches of it looking at me
Is this the place, we used to love
Is this the place that I've been dreaming of

Oh! Simple thing where have you gone
I'm getting old and I need something to rely on
So tell me when you're gonna let me in
I'm getting tired and I need somewhere to begin

And If you have a minute why don't we go
Talking about that somewhere only we know?
This could be the end of everything
So why don't we go
Somewhere only we know?
(Somewhere only we know)

Oh! Simple thing where have you gone
I'm getting old and I need something to rely on
So tell me when you gonna let me in
I'm getting tired and I need somewhere to begin

And If you have a minute why don't we go
Talking about that somewhere only we know?
This could be the end of everything
So why don't we go
So why don't we go

This could be the end of everything
So why don't we go
Somewhere only we know?
Somewhere only we know?
Somewhere only we know?

You gotta be

Des'ree

INFORMAÇÕES TÉCNICAS

Composição: Des'ree
Estilo: Pop
Cantora: Des'ree
Site oficial: www.desree.co.uk
Tema: Motivacional, viva seu dia

Informações sobre a cantora e a música

Desirée Annette Weeks é uma cantora e compositora inglesa nascida em Barbados em 1968. Ela foi muito popular nos anos 90. Sua música "You gotta be" foi lançada em 1994 e faz parte do álbum *I ain't moving*. Ela foi escolhida para fazer parte de um álbum em tributo à princesa Diana.

Teaching tips

Esta atividade pode ser usada para introduzir ou reforçar o uso da forma comparativa. Inicie a aula pedindo aos alunos que leiam os primeiros versos e a partir deles deduzam qual é o tema da música. Durante o *Listening* os alunos ouvem a música e completam os versos com os adjetivos. Se necessário, explique o uso de *gotta* (britânico) que substitui *got to (have to)*. Na atividade seguinte peça aos alunos que observem a forma dos adjetivos e retirem dois que estão sendo usados como comparativos. Para fazer a atividade 3, leia as palavras em voz alta e peça aos alunos para repeti-las. Em seguida toque a música para que eles encontrem palavras que rimam. Você pode pedir que digam palavras conhecidas que rimam com as palavras dadas antes de ouvir a música.

No *After listening*, organize a classe em pares para que os alunos formem o comparativo dos adjetivos dados e escrevam sentenças com eles.

Answer key

Before listening

1. Open answer. Suggestion:
   Seize the day.

Listening

1. You gotta be <u>bad</u>   You gotta be <u>bold</u>
   You gotta be <u>wiser</u>   You gotta be <u>hard</u>
   You gotta be <u>tough</u>   You gotta be <u>stronger</u>
   You gotta be <u>cool</u>   You gotta be <u>calm</u>

2. a) wiser
   b) stronger

3. a) cheers: tears, fears
   b) my: sky, cry
   c) lace: pace, face
   d) led: said, read
   e) molds: unfolds, holds

After listening

1. Open answers.
   a) bad (worse)
   b) calm (calmer)
   c) hard (harder)
   d) cool (cooler)
   e) bold (bolder)

Lyrics

"You gotta be"

Listen as your day unfolds
Challenge what the future holds
Try and keep your head up to the sky
Lovers, they may cause you tears
Go ahead release your fears
Stand up and be counted
Don't be ashamed to cry
You gotta be...
You gotta be bad, you gotta be bold, you gotta be wiser
You gotta be hard, you gotta be tough, you gotta be stronger
You gotta be cool, you gotta be calm, you gotta stay together
All I know, all I know, love will save the day
Herald what your mother said
Read the books your father read
Try to solve the puzzles in your own sweet time
Some may have more cash than you
Others take a different view
My oh my, yea, eh, ee
Time ask no questions, it goes on without you
Leaving you behind if you can't stand the pace
The world keeps on spinning
Can't stop it, if you tried to
This best part is danger staring you in the face

Listen to your heart

The Maine

INFORMAÇÕES TÉCNICAS

Composição: Gene MacLellan
Estilo: Pop rock
Integrantes: Pat Kirch, Garrett Nickelsen, John O'Callaghan, Kennedy Brock e Jared Monaco.
Site oficial: http://www.wearethemaine.net/splash/
Tema: Amor na adolescência

Informações sobre a banda e a música

Quando a banda The Maine foi formada em 2007, a maior parte dos membros ainda estava cursando o Ensino Médio. O nome The Maine surgiu a partir de uma música chamada "Coast of Maine" do Ivory, que é uma das influências musicais da banda.

Teaching tips

Para o *Before listening* organize a classe em pares e sugira que conversem a respeito das quatro primeiras questões. Abra a discussão para a classe toda. Dependendo do nível de sua turma use a língua alvo (inglês) todo o tempo. Explique o objetivo da primeira questão do *Listening* antes de ouvir a música. Ouçam a música juntos e reforce que os alunos devem justificar suas respostas escrevendo o verso correspondente à sentença dada.

Na segunda atividade, leia em voz alta e repita as palavras dadas. Os alunos terão mais facilidade para fazer o exercício. Peça-lhes que batam palmas quando ouvirem uma palavra que rima. Pare a música e peça que escrevam a palavra no quadro. Repita esse procedimento até que o quadro esteja completo. Duran-te o *After listening*, os alunos devem trocar ideias com seus pares a respeito do tema da música e, em seguida, escrever individualmente suas opiniões. Mostre o vídeo sugerido e peça que cantem a música, se achar apropriado.

Answer key

Before listening

1. Open answers.

Listening

1. a) (F) Your father he says I'm not good enough.
    b) (T) Your mother she thinks that this is just a phase.
    c) (F) Don't listen to your friends.
    d) (F) Listen to your heart.

2.

line	mine	time
smart	start	apart
proud	loud	crowd
she	me	free

After listening

1. Open answer.

2. Watch the video clip and sing together.

Lyrics

"Listen to your heart"

We're too young
This is never gonna work
That's what they say
You are gonna get hurt
But I know something they don't
I hear you heart beating right in time
Right from the start I knew I had to make you mine
And now, I'll never let you go
Don't they know love won't lie
Don't listen to the world
They say we're never gonna make it
Don't listen to your friends
They would've never let us start
And don't listen to the voices in your head
Listen to your heart
This promise, doesn't have to be too loud
Just whisper I can find you in a crowd
I think it's time we ran away
Your father
He says I'm not good enough then
Your mother she thinks that this is just a phase
I think that we should run away
Don't listen to the world
They say we'll never gonna make it
Don't listen to your friends
They would've never let us start
And don't listen to the voices in your head
Listen to your heart
You gotta listen to your heart
Come on and listen to your heart.
It will tell the truth
It will set you free
It will say that you were meant for me
And this is where we supposed to be, yeah

Don't listen to the world
They say we're never gonna make it
But I'm the one make it
Don't listen to your friends
They would've never let us start
And don't listen to the voices in your head
Love will never ever let us fall apart
You gotta listen to your heart
Come on and listen to your heart
You gotta listen to your heart
Come on and listen to your heart

Better days

Goo Goo Dolls

INFORMAÇÕES TÉCNICAS

Composição: Goo Goo Dolls

Estilo: Rock alternativo

Integrantes: Johnny Rzeznik (vocais e guitarras), Robby Takac (baixo e vocais), e Mike Malinin (substituto de George Tutuska na bateria)

Site oficial: http://www.googoodolls.com

Tema: resoluções de Ano Novo, Natal

Informações sobre a banda e a música

Goo Goo Dolls é uma banda de rock alternativo dos Estados Unidos, formada em 1986, em Buffalo. "Better days" foi lançada em 2005 no álbum *Let love in*.

Teaching tips

Esta é uma atividade de quinze minutos que pode ser usada como um *warm up*. Durante o *Before listening* organize a classe em pares e peça aos alunos que respondam as perguntas. Em seguida eles devem ler a primeira atividade do *Listening* antes de ouvir a música. Dessa forma farão a atividade com mais objetividade. Os alunos ouvem a música e assinalam *True* ou *False* e reescrevem as sentenças falsas. Peça-lhes que corrijam a atividade com seus pares.

Na segunda atividade, os alunos relacionam as palavras que rimam. Leia e faça *repetition* das palavras, reforçando os sons que rimam. Coloque a música novamente e peça aos alunos que batam palmas ao ouvir as palavras. Esse é um bom exercício de *listening* com um objetivo bem definido. Entregue a letra da música para os alunos para que façam as demais atividades com base na leitura. Corrija as questões. Durante o *After listening* os alunos vão escrever duas sentenças usando *Next year I'm going to... I want... for Christmas*.

Answer key

Before listening

1. Open answers

Listening

1. (F) Everyone is forgiven now.
   (F) Tonight the world begins.
   (F) Everybody should have a simple place to live.
   (T) You can give faith, trust and peace.
   (T) You can say a prayer to the poor children.

2. year — clear; live — give; tonight — fight; strings — things; now — loud

3. Listen to the song and clap your hands every time you hear the words above.

4. Yes. *And the one poor Child that saved this world* (referring to Jesus Christ); *'cause I don't need boxes wrapped in strings* (referring to gifts you get on Christmas).

5. *Just a chance that maybe we'll find better days.*

After listening

Open answers:
a) Next year I'm going to...
b) I want... for Christmas.

Lyrics

"Better days"

And you ask me what I want this year
And I try to make this kind and clear
Just a chance that maybe we'll find better days
'cause I don't need boxes wrapped in strings
And desire and love and empty things
Just a chance that maybe we'll find better days
So take these words
And sing out loud
'cause everyone is forgiven now
'cause tonight's the night the world begins again.
And it's someplace simple where we could live
And something only you can give
And that's faith and trust and peace while we're alive
And the one poor Child that saved this world
And there's 10 million more who probably could
If we all just stopped and said a prayer for them.
So take these words
And sing out loud
'cause everyone is forgiven now
'cause tonight's the night the world begins again.
I wish everyone was loved tonight
And somehow stop this endless fight
Just a chance that maybe we'll find better days
So take these words
And sing out loud
'cause everyone is forgiven now
'cause tonight's the night the world begins again
'cause tonight's the night the world begins again.

Rehab

Amy Winehouse

INFORMAÇÕES TÉCNICAS

Composição: Amy Winehouse
Estilo: Soul/jazz
Cantora: Amy Winehouse
Site oficial: http://www.amywinehouse.com/
Tema: Reabilitação, consumo de drogas ilícitas, dependência química

Informações sobre a cantora e a música

"Rehab" é uma canção escrita por Amy Winehouse, para o seu segundo álbum de estúdio, *Back to black*, de 2006. A letra é autobiográfica. É o mais premiado *hit* da cantora. Ganhou o Grammy de melhor canção no MTV Europe Music Awards, gravação do ano no MTV Video Music Awards e melhor música conteporânea no Ivor Novello Awards. Amy Winehouse faleceu em 2011 aos 27 anos. Morreu jovem como outros cantores famosos: Janis Joplin, Kurt Cobain e Jimmi Hendrix.

Teaching tips

Converse com seus alunos a respeito do uso de drogas, dependência química e reabilitação. Levante o conhecimento prévio que eles têm sobre o assunto. Escreva na lousa: *different kinds of addiction* e faça um levantamento com os alunos sobre o tema. Organize a classe em pares para que respondam à primeira pergunta. Em seguida, distribua a letra da música para que respondam às perguntas 2 e 3. Peça que primeiramente leiam as perguntas e depois façam a leitura com mais objetividade. Explique a pergunta 3, dizendo que eles podem levantar hipóteses sobre o significado das expressões baseando-se no contexto. Peça-lhes que interajam entre pares para comparar suas respostas. Corrija as respostas das atividades 2 e 3 comparando as diversas hipóteses levantadas pelos alunos.

Ouça a música com os alunos para fazer a atividade sobre rimas. Em seguida, peça que releiam a letra da música sublinhando os verbos no *simple past* e no *present perfect* e preencham o quadro. Os alunos devem escrever um parágrafo sobre a cantora utilizando alguns dos verbos do quadro para finalizar a atividade.

Answer key

Before listening

1. An addiction is the habitual compulsion to use a substance, or to engage in an activity without much regard for its detrimental effects on a person's physical, mental, financial, social and spiritual well-being. Examples of different kinds of addiction: alcohol, drug, nicotine, food, gambling, sex, porn, video game, shopping, exercise, work etc.

2. a) She says she has no time.
    b) He thinks she's fine but he wants her to go to rehab.
    c) 70 days, ten weeks.
    d) She'd rather be at home with Ray.

3. **"I've been black":** I've been depressed, down.

    "a shot glass": it is a small glass designed to hold or measure spirits or liquor, which is either drunk straight from the glass ("a shot") or poured into a mixed drink.

    "I'm on the mend": I'm recovering, getting better (after being sick).

Listening

1. know: no, go
   time: fine
   Ray: Hathaway
   friend: mend
   class: glass
   dried: pride
   here: near
   black: back

After listening

1.

Simple past	Present Perfect
tried	have been
didn't get, got	has tried
said	have dried

2. Suggestion: Amy Winehouse tried to get rid of her addiction. She said she didn't want to go to rehab. She tried to stop drinking but she wasn't successful. She was 27 when she died.

Lyrics

"Rehab"

They tried to make me go to rehab but I said 'no, no, no'
Yes, I've been black but when I come back, you'll know, know, know.
I ain't got the time and if my daddy thinks I'm fine,
He's tried to make me go to rehab, but I won't go, go, go.

I'd rather be at home with Ray,
I ain't got seventy days

'Cause there's nothing,
There's nothing you can teach me
That I can't learn from Mr. Hathaway.

I didn't get a lot in class,
But I know it don't come in a shot glass.

They tried to make me go to rehab but I said 'no, no, no'
Yes, I've been black but when I come back you'll know, know, know.
I ain't got the time and if my daddy thinks I'm fine,
He's tried to make me go to rehab but I won't go go go.

The man said 'why do you think you're here'
I said 'I got no idea
I'm gonna, I'm gonna lose my babe
so I always keep a bottle near'
He said 'I just think you're depressed,
this is me, yeah babe, and the rest'

They tried to make me go to rehab but I said 'no, no, no'
Yes, I've been black but when I come back you'll know, know, know.

I don't ever wanna drink again,
I just need a friend
I'm not gonna spend ten weeks,
have everyone think I'm on the mend.

It's not just my pride,
It's just 'til these tears have dried.

They tried to make me go to rehab but I said 'no, no, no'
Yes, I've been black but when I come back you'll know, know, know.
I ain't got the time and if my daddy thinks I'm fine
He's tried to make me go to rehab but I won't go, go, go.

I don't wanna miss a thing

Aerosmith

INFORMAÇÕES TÉCNICAS

Composição: Diane Warren

Estilo: Rock, Hard Rock, Heavy Metal,

Integrantes: Steven Tyler, Joe Perry, Brad Whitford, Tom Hamilton e Joey Kramer

Site oficial: www.aerosmith.com

Tema: Amor

Informações sobre a banda e a música

"I don't want to miss a thing" é um *hit-single* da banda norte-americana de rock Aerosmith. Ele foi lançado a partir da trilha sonora do filme *Armageddon*. Em novembro de 1998 esse hit tornou-se a canção do Aerosmith com mais alta posição na parada musical do Reino Unido até então.

Teaching tips

Comece perguntando aos alunos se eles gostam de rock e que tipo de rock eles gostam. Sugira que mencionem suas bandas preferidas. Em seguida, faça as perguntas do *Before listening*. Peça aos alunos que pensem em outras músicas que usem essas contrações *wanna, gonna etc.*

Durante o *Listening*, peça aos alunos que leiam a atividade antes de ouvir a música para que eles a escutem com objetivos claros.

Na atividade do *After listening* os alunos devem pensar em outros verbos que são usados coloquialmente e não podem ser usados no inglês formal.

Answer key

Before listening

1. "Love of my life" (Queen), "Wish you were here" (Pink Floyd), "Have you ever loved a woman?" (Brian Adams) e outros.

2. The Police, *"Every little thing she does is magic"*: *Everything she do just* Timbaland, *"The way I are"*: *Can you handle me the way I are?* e outras...

3. The use of the verb *wanna*.

Listening

1. Breathing, sleeping, dreaming, laying, feeling, beating.

2. Example: Yesterday while I was sleeping, I could hear my heart beating. I was feeling very tired.

3. *Every moment spent with you*
    Is a moment of treasure
    Then I kiss your eyes and thank God we're together

After listening

1. Gotta, dunno

2. Open answers.

Lyrics

"I don't want to miss a thing"

I could stay awake just to hear you breathing
Watch you smile while you are sleeping
While you're far away and dreaming
I could spend my life in this sweet surrender
I could stay lost in this moment forever
Every moment spent with you
Is a moment of treasure
Don't wanna close my eyes
I don't wanna fall asleep
'Cause I'd miss you baby
And I don't wanna miss a thing
'Cause even when I dream of you
The sweetest dream would never do
I'd still miss you baby
And I don't wanna miss a thing
Laying close to you
Feeling your heart beating
And I'm wondering what you're dreaming
Wondering if it's me you're seeing
Then I kiss your eyes and thank God we're together
And I just want to stay with you
In this moment forever, forever and ever
Don't wanna close my eyes
I don't wanna fall asleep
'Cause I'd miss you, baby
And I don't wanna miss a thing
'Cause even when I dream of you
The sweetest dream will never do
I'd still miss you, baby
And I don't wanna miss a thing
I don't wanna miss one smile
I don't wanna miss one kiss
I just wanna be with you
Right here with you, just like this

I just wanna hold you close
I feel your heart so close to mine
And just stay here in this moment
For all the rest of time
Yeah, yeah, yeah, yeah, yeah!
Don't wanna close my eyes
I don't wanna fall a sleep
'Cause I'd miss you, baby
And I don't wanna miss a thing
'Cause even when I dream of you
The sweetest dream will never do
I'd still miss you, baby
And I don't wanna miss a thing
Don't wanna close my eyes
I don't wanna fall a sleep
'Cause I'd miss you, baby
And I don't wanna miss a thing
'Cause even when I dream of you
The sweetest dream will never do
I'd still miss you, baby
And I don't wanna miss a thing
Don't wanna close my eyes
Don't wanna fall asleep, yeah
I don't want to miss a thing

Come home soon

Corey Crowder

INFORMAÇÕES TÉCNICAS

Composição: Corey Crowder
Estilo: Soul music
Cantor: Corey Crowder
Site oficial: http://www.coreycrowder.net/
Tema: Amor, saudade

Informações sobre o cantor e a música

Jonathan Corey Crowder é um jovem cantor e compositor americano nascido na Georgia. "Come home soon" pertence ao álbum *Learning to let go* (2005).

Teaching tips

Durante o *Before listening*, organize a classe em pares e peça às duplas que respondam às perguntas da primeira atividade. Em seguida deixe que os alunos relatem o que ouviram. Você poderá conhecer um pouco mais sobre os gostos musicais de seus alunos e dessa forma escolher as próximas atividades. Na segunda atividade eles devem completar as sentenças individualmente e compará-las com as de seus colegas. Eles devem escolher uma sentença de cada um para relatar para a classe. As melhores podem ser organizadas em um mural. O objetivo das atividades do *Listening* é lexical (rimas e vocabulário). Durante o *After listening*, os alunos completarão as sentenças que contêm expressões retiradas da letra da música. Peça-lhes que observem o significado das sentenças na música antes de fazer a atividade.

Answer key

Before listening

1. Open answers.

2. Open answers.

3. Open answer.

Listening

1.

behind	kind	mind	rewind
May	day	say	pay
bride	side	hide	pride
spring	thing	sing	king
sheep	keep	deep	creap

2. Listen to the song and find related words.

tomorrow	today	yesterday	week	calendar	time

3. Listen to the song again and find opposite words.

with	without
shallow	deep
low	high
outside	inside
different	same
there	here

After listening

1. Open answers.

2. Open answers.

Lyrics

"Come home soon"

It has the makings of the next big thing.
There's a time to mourn and a time to sing.
Is there a reason why we're here?
It's been a week since you've been gone
and I could swear the calendar is wrong.
My back is against the wall.
Without you here at my side it's not the same from day to day.
I can't bear to hide the words that I've refused to say.
You see, I've found that I'm lost without you around.
I miss you, so come home soon.
Love is patient, love is kind.
And with that said keep this in mind.
There's nothing you can do to stop the flame that burns inside.
No valley deep, no mountain high.
Yesterday, today the same.
Without you here at my side it's not the same from day to day.
I can't bear to hide the words that I've refused to say.
You see, I've found that I'm lost without you around.
I miss you, so come home soon.
I miss you, so come home soon, come home soon.

Another brick in the wall

Pink Floyd

INFORMAÇÕES TÉCNICAS

Composição: Roger Waters
Estilo: Psicodelia, progressivo, rock
Integrantes: Syd Barrett, Rick Wright, Roger Waters, Nick Mason e David Gilmour
Site oficial: www.pinkfloyd.com
Tema: Educação

Informações sobre a banda e a música

Pink Floyd foi uma banda de rock britânica formada em Cambridge, Inglaterra, em 1965. A banda é muito conhecida por sua música progressiva com uso de letras filosóficas, experimentações musicais, capas de álbuns inovadoras e shows elaborados. O Pink Floyd é um dos grupos de rock mais comercialmente bem-sucedido da história, tendo vendido mais de 300 milhões de álbuns.

"Another brick in the wall" é uma faixa do álbum *The wall*. A música é muito conhecida por sua frase "We don't need no education..." e foi um dos maiores *hits* da banda, alcançando o primeiro lugar das paradas no mundo. Ela é basicamente uma crítica ao rígido sistema educacional, especialmente de internatos. No Brasil, chegou a ser a segunda canção mais tocada nas rádios em 1980.

Teaching tips

Converse com os alunos a respeito de sua educação escolar. Use as perguntas do *Before listening* para contextualizar o tema. Explore bastante o tópico comparando a educação de hoje com a educação de quarenta anos atrás. Se estiver trabalhando com jovens em idade escolar pergunte como é sua relação com seus professores hoje. Em seguida peça a eles que observem o quadro da primeira atividade do *Listening* e verifiquem os títulos de cada coluna. Quais palavras eles imaginam que podem aparecer na música e que se encaixam nessas colunas? Coloque a música e peça que preencham o quadro. Corrija com eles. Na segunda atividade peça que ouçam a segunda parte da música e pergunte a eles se concordam com a letra. Ressalte a construção gramatical das primeiras duas sentenças e explique que é uma construção informal usando o *double negative* que não deve ser usado formalmente.

> We don't need no education
> We don't need no thought control
> No dark sarcasm in the classroom
> Teachers leave them kids alone
> Hey! Teachers! Leave them kids alone!
> All in all it's just another brick in the wall.
> All in all you're just another brick in the wall.

Pergunte a eles se acham que a educação escolar é importante, se eles concordam com esses versos, e o que a escola pode fazer de diferente para que eles não se sintam apenas mais um número na sala de aula. Na atividade de *After listening* divida os alunos em grupos de três para que façam uma lista de todos os adjetivos que podem ser usados para descrever uma escola. A ideia é que descrevam a escola ideal escrevendo no local indicado. Em seguida peça que reportem para a classe.

Answer key

Before listening

1. Open answer.

2. Open answer.

3. Open answer.

Listening

1.

Words related to school	Words related to people
School, teachers, children, expose, weakness, kids	Fat, daddy, memory, wives, psychopathic

2. Open answer

3. Open answer.

After listening

1. Friendly environment, strict environment, well equipped, big, small, friendly teachers, subjects.

2. Open answer.

Lyrics

"Another brick in the wall"

Parte 1

Daddy's flown across the ocean
Leaving just a memory
Snapshot in the family album
Daddy what else did you leave for me?
Daddy, what'd'ja leave behind for me?!?
All in all it was just a brick in the wall.
All in all it was all just bricks in the wall.

"You! Yes, you behind the bikesheds, stand still
lady!"

When we grew up and went to school
There were certain teachers who would
Hurt the children in any way they could
(oof!)
By pouring their derision
Upon anything we did
And exposing every weakness
However carefully hidden by the kids
But in the town it was well known
When they got home at night, their fat and
Psychopathic wives would thrash them
Within inches of their lives.

Parte 2

We don't need no education
We don't need no thought control
No dark sarcasm in the classroom
Teachers leave them kids alone
Hey! Teachers! Leave them kids alone!
All in all it's just another brick in the wall.
All in all you're just another brick in the wall.

We don't need no education
We don't need no thought control
No dark sarcasm in the classroom
Teachers leave us kids alone
Hey! Teachers! Leave us kids alone!
All in all it's just another brick in the wall.
All in all you're just another brick in the wall.

"Wrong, Guess again! 2x
If you don't eat yer meat, you can't have any pudding.
How can you have any pudding if you don't eat yer meat?
You! Yes, you behind the bikesheds, stand still laddie!"

Parte 3

I don't need no arms around me
And I don't need no drugs to calm me
I have seen the writing on the wall
Don't think I need anything at all

No! Don't think I'll need anything at all
All in all it was all just bricks in the wall.
All in all you were all just bricks in the wall.

Earth song

Michael Jackson

INFORMAÇÕES TÉCNICAS

Composição: Michael Jackson
Estilo: Blues, Gospel
Cantor: Michael Jackson
Site oficial: www.michaeljackson.com
Tema: Ecologia, desmatamento

Informação sobre o cantor e a música

Michael Joseph Jackson nasceu em Gary no dia 29 de agosto de 1958 e faleceu em Los Angeles no dia 25 de junho de 2009. Cantor, compositor, dançarino, produtor, empresário e arranjador vocal muito importante no contexto musical americano. Segundo a revista *Rolling Stone,* faturou em vida cerca de 7 bilhões de dólares e um ano após sua morte suas músicas faturaram cerca de 1 bilhão de dólares. Começou a cantar e a dançar aos cinco anos de idade, iniciando sua carreira profissional aos onze anos como vocalista da Jackson 5, banda formada com seus irmãos. Em 1971, começou sua carreira solo, sendo logo reconhecido como o Rei do Pop. *Earth Song* foi escrita por Jackson na década de 1990. A canção tem um clima de música clássica. Nessa música, Jackson alerta para a consciência social, avisando que estamos indo longe demais com nossas atitudes para com o planeta Terra. A canção foi indicada ao Grammy em 1997. Jackson recebeu um Prêmio Gênesis por *Earth song* e a canção foi usada em um comercial de TV que alertava para os riscos ambientais.

Teaching tips

Faça as perguntas indicadas no *Before listening* para contextualizar o assunto. Explore o tópico perguntando aos alunos se eles acham que a humanidade está acabando com as florestas e a ecologia. Coloque o clipe para que os alunos assistam. Se não for possível peça que ouçam somente a música. Eles devem estar atentos às palavras indicadas e bater palmas ao escutá-las. Em seguida, peça-lhes que escrevam um parágrafo a respeito do assunto, mostrando se eles estão de acordo com a letra da música ou não.

Answer key

Before listening

1. Open answer.

2. Open answer.

3. Open answer

4. Open answer.

Listening

1. Open answer.

2. Open answer.

After listening

1. Open answer.

Lyrics

"Earth song"

What about sunrise
What about rain
What about all the things
That you said we were to gain
What about killing fields
Is there a time
What about all the things
That you said was yours and mine
Did you ever stop to notice
All the blood we've shed before
Did you ever stop to notice
This crying Earth, its' weeping shore
Aaaaaaaaah Oooooooooh
Aaaaaaaaah Oooooooooh
What have we've done to the world
Look what we've done
What about all the peace
That you pledge your only son
What about flowering fields
Is there a time
What about all the dreams
That you said was yours and mine
Did you ever stop to notice
All the children dead from war
Did you ever stop to notice
This crying Earth, its' weeping shore
Aaaaaaaaah Oooooooooh
Aaaaaaaaah Oooooooooh
I used to dream
I used to glance beyond the stars
Now I don't know where we are
Although I know we've drifted far
Aaaaaaaaah Oooooooooh
Aaaaaaaaah Oooooooooh

Aaaaaaaaah Ooooooooh
Aaaaaaaaah Ooooooooh
Hey, what about yesterday
(What about us)
What about the seas
(What about us)
Heavens are falling down
(What about us)
I can't even breathe
(What about us)
What about apathy
(What about us)
I need you
(What about us)
What about nature's worth
(ooo, ooo)
It's our planet's womb
(What about us)
What about animals
(What about it)
Turn kingdom to dust
(What about us)
What about elephants
(What about us)
Have we lost their trust
(What about us)
What about crying whales
(What about us)
Ravaging the seas
(What about us)
What about forest trails
(ooo, ooo)
Burnt despite our pleas
(What about us)
What about the holy land
(What about it)
Torn apart by greed
(What about us)

What about the common man
(What about us)
Can't we set him free
(What about us)
What about children dying
(What about us)
Can't you hear them cry
(What about us)
Where did we go wrong
(ooo, ooo)
Someone tell me why
(What about us)
What about baby boy
(What about it)
What about the days
(What about us)
What about all their joy
(What about us)
What about the man
(What about us)
What about the crying man
(What about us)
What about Abraham
(What about us)
What about death again
(ooo, ooo)
Do we give a damn

Into the West

Annie Lennox

INFORMAÇÕES TÉCNICAS

Composição: Fran Walsh, Howard Shore e Annie Lennox
Estilo: Soul
Cantora: Annie Lennox
Site oficial: http://www.annielennox.com/
Tema: Morte

Informações sobre a cantora e a música

Annie Lennox é uma premiada cantora e compositora escocesa. Foi vocalista do grupo Eurythmics. A música "Into the West" ganhou o Oscar de Melhor Canção Original, um dos onze prêmios que o filme *O senhor dos anéis* conquistou em 2004. Annie sempre foi engajada em causas sociais e, em 2009, ela criou sua própria campanha chamada Sing, destinada a apoiar mulheres e crianças víti-mas do vírus HIV no continente africano.

Muitos versos da música foram retirados do último capítulo do livro terceiro da trilogia: *O senhor dos anéis – O retorno do rei*. O diretor Peter Jackson explica que a música foi parcialmente inspirada pelo jovem cineasta Cameron Duncan, que morreu de câncer prematuramente, e cujo trabalho impressionou Jackson e sua equipe. A primeira representação pública da música foi no funeral desse cineasta.

Teaching tips

As atividades do *Before listening* são de leitura. Entregue a letra da música aos alunos, organize-os em pares e peça que leiam somente a primeira estrofe. Eles devem deduzir o tema da música a partir dessa primeira estrofe. A próxima etapa é ler toda a letra, procurando outras sentenças que transmitam a mesma ideia da primeira estrofe. Para fazer as atividades de *Listening*, peça a os alunos que guardem a letra da música. Na primeira atividade de Listening, os alunos escrevem palavras relacionadas com *life* e *death*, ouvidas na música. Peça a eles que acrescentem uma palavra relacionada à vida e à morte que seja significativa para eles. As palavras podem variar. Os alunos devem comparar suas respostas com seus pares e em seguida com toda a classe. As palavras podem ser colocadas na lousa. Na segunda atividade eles preencherão o quadro com os tempos verbais sugeridos. Observe e reforce que nem todo o quadro será preenchido e chame a atenção para os exemplos. Esse pode ser um bom momento para uma revisão de tempos verbais. Durante o *After listening*, os alunos vão escolher duas dessas palavras e dois tempos verbais e escrever sentenças a respeito de *life* e *death*. Na última atividade os alunos escrevem sua interpretação da letra da música.

Answer key

Before listening

1. Open answer. Suggestion: death.

2. All of your fears will pass away, safe in my arms, you're only sleeping.
    The ships have come to carry you home.
    We have come now to the end.

Listening

1. Open answer. Suggestions:
    life: light, dream, fears, before, memory, time
    death: night, sleep, journey's end, moon, hope, home

Present Continuous	Simple past	Present perfect	Imperative	Future
is falling	came	have come	lay down	will see
are calling			sleep	will pass away
are sleeping			dream	will turn
			don't say	will meet
				will be

After listening

1. Open answers.

2. Open answer.

Lyrics

"Into the West"

Lay down
Your sweet and weary head
The night is falling
You have come to journey's end
Sleep now
And dream of the ones who came before
They are calling
From across the distant shore

Why do you weep?
What are these tears upon your face?
Soon you will see
All of your fears will pass away
Safe in my arms
You're only sleeping

What can you see
On the horizon?
Why do the white gulls call?
Across the sea
A pale moon rises
The ships have come to carry you home

And all will turn
To silver glass
A light on the water
All souls pass

Hope fades
Into the world of night
Through shadows falling
Out of memory and time
Don't say
We have come now to the end
White shores are calling
You and I will meet again
And you'll be here in my arms
Just sleeping

(Chorus)

And all will turn
To silver glass
A light on the water
Grey ships pass into the west

What kind of world do you want?

Five For Fighting

INFORMAÇÕES TÉCNICAS

Composição: John Ondrasik
Estilo: Rock, Pop rock
Cantor: John Ondrasik
Site oficial: http://www.fiveforfighting.com
Tema: Que tipo de mundo você quer?

Informações sobre o cantor e a música

Five for Fighting é o nome artístico usado pelo cantor e compositor americano John Ondrasik. Em 2007, foi criado o site *What Kind Of World Do You Want?* Seu objetivo é levantar fundos para várias instituições diferentes. No site os fãs podem fazer *upload* de vídeos respondendo à pergunta: "Que tipo de mundo você quer?"

Teaching tips

Essa canção deve ser usada como um *warm up* antes de uma aula que se refere a mudanças no mundo ou o que as pessoas esperam do mundo. Peça aos alunos que se sentem em pares e respondam à primeira pergunta do *Before listening*, fazendo uma lista sobre o que eles esperam desse mundo.

Em seguida os alunos devem ler as duas perguntas do *Listening*. Coloque a música para que eles ouçam e respondam. Para responderem à terceira e à quarta pergunta entregue a música por escrito e peça a eles que procurem as respostas. Na quinta pergunta eles devem ouvir a música e completar com o verbo. Não deixe que leiam a música para essa questão. Em seguida, divida a classe em trios e peça a eles que discutam as duas perguntas do *After listening*. Cada trio deve reportar suas ideias a todo o grupo.

Answer key

Before listening

1. Open answer.

Listening

1. Package full of wishes, a time machine, a magic wand, a globe made out of gold.

2. Open answer.

3. Let's start at the start, build a masterpiece.

4. Sunlight, earthquake and oceans.

5. a) Take a chance
    b) Grab a piece
    c) Build a masterpiece
    d) Raise your army
    e) Look the other way
    f) Think anything
    g) Fill the oceans

After listening

1. Open answer.

2. Suggested answers: nuclear bombs, cloning, robots, destruction of nature, asteroid collision.

Lyrics

"What kind of world do you want?"

Got a package full of wishes
A Time machine, a magic wand, a globe made out of gold
No instructions or commandments,
Laws of gravity or indecisions to uphold

Printed on the box I see,
ACME's built a world to be,
Take a chance, grab a piece,
Help me to believe it

What kind of world do you want?
Think anything
Let's start at the start, build a masterpiece,
Be careful what you wish for
History starts now

Should there be people or peoples?
Money, funny, pedestals, for fools who never pay
Raise your army, choose you steeple
Don't be shy, the satellites, can look the other way

Lose the earthquakes, keep the faults
Fill the oceans, without the salt
Let every man own his own hand
Can you dig it baby?

What kind of world do you want?
Think anything
Let's start at the start, build a masterpiece,

Be careful what you wish for
History starts now

Sunlight's on the bridge
Sunlight's on the way
Tomorrow's calling
There's more to this than love

What kind of world do you want?
What kind of world do you want?

What kind of world do you want?
Think anything
Let's start at the start, build a masterpiece, yeah
History starts now, starts now

Be careful what you wish for

Start now, now.

Crying shame

Jack Johnson

INFORMAÇÕES TÉCNICAS

Compositor: Jack Johnson
Estilo: Folk, Pop rock
Site oficial: www.jackjohnsonmusic.com
Tema: Guerra

Informações sobre o cantor e a música

Jack Hody Johnson nasceu em Honolulu, Havaí, e atualmente vive em Haleiwa. Antes de lançar seu primeiro álbum de estúdio, Jack Johnson fazia filmes sobre surfe. Ele estudou cinema na Califórnia. Em 2010, Johnson fez uma grande turnê pelos Estados Unidos, Canadá, Europa e Ásia. No começo de 2011, ele anunciou que faria oito shows no Brasil (São Paulo, Belo Horizonte, Brasília, Fortaleza, Recife, Porto Alegre, Florianópolis e Rio de Janeiro).

Teaching tips

Coloque a palavra *WAR* na lousa. Peça a cada aluno que fale uma palavra que venha à mente relacionada à palavra WAR. Todos os alunos devem dizer uma palavra em inglês. Coloque essas palavras na lousa também. Contextualize o tópico fazendo as perguntas do *Before listening*. Na primeira questão do *Listening* peça aos alunos que primeiramente leiam a atividade para ouvir a música com o objetivo definido. Eles devem responder com verdadeiro ou falso, justificando-as com versos da música. Novamente, peça a eles que leiam as sentenças da segunda questão antes de ouvir a música. Eles deverão achar um verso na música com o mesmo significado da frase. Termine com as perguntas do *After listening*.

Answer key

Before listening

1. Open answer.

2. Open answer.

3. Open answer.

Listening

1. (F) He thinks we communicate well. <u>We should know how to communicate</u>
   (F) It is difficult to control the world now. <u>We're on a roll and there ain't no stopping us now</u>.
   (F) He believes someone wins and someone loses. <u>We could try but nobody wins</u>.
   (T) War uses fear as fuel.
   (T) There is no one to blame.

2. Find a verse that means:

   a) By now we should know how to communicate.
   b) We're all burning under the same sun.
   c) A number of people are numbers that aren't coming home.
   d) We could close our eyes it's still there.
   e) Using fear as fuel.
   f) Are we losing what we were?
   g) And how will this all play out?

After listening

1. Open answer.

2. Open answer.

Lyrics

"Crying shame"

It's such a tired game
Will it ever stop?
How will this all play out
Out of sight, out of mind
By now we should know how to communicate
Instead of coming to blows
We're on a roll
And there ain't no stopping us now
We're burning under control
Isn't it strange how we're all burning under the same sun?
Buy now and save, it's a war for peace
It's the same old game
But do we really want to play?
We could close our eyes it's still there
We could say it's us against them
We could try but nobody wins
Gravity has got a hold on us all
We could try to put it out, but it's a growing flame
Using fear as fuel
Burning down our name
And it won't take too long
'Cause words all burn the same
And who are we going to blame now?
It's such a crying, crying, crying shame
By now it's beginning to show
A number of people are numbers that aren't coming home
I could close my eyes it's still there
Close my mind be alone
I could close my heart and not care
But gravity has got a hold on us all
It's a terrific price to pay
But in the true sense of the word
Are we using what we've learned?
But in the true sense of the word

Are we losing what we were?
It's such a tired game
Will it ever stop?
It's not for me to say
Is it in our blood or is it in our fate?
And how will this all play out?
Out of sight, out of mind
Who are we going to blame all in all?
It's just a crying, crying, crying shame.

That I would be good

Alanis Morissette

INFORMAÇÕES TÉCNICAS

Composição: Alanis Morissette
Estilo: Pop
Cantora: Alanis Morissette
Site oficial: http://www.alanis.com/
Tema: Otimismo perante adversidades

Informações sobre a cantora e a música

Alanis Nadine Morissette (Ottawa, 1 de junho de 1974) é uma cantora, compositora, produtora e atriz canadense, vencedora de treze Junos e sete Grammys. Desde 1991 já vendeu cerca de 72 milhões de cópias em todo o mundo. Alanis foi a cantora mais bem-sucedida na década de 1990 e, em 2002, era uma das cantoras mais bem pagas do mundo.

Teaching tips

Inicie a aula dividindo a classe em duplas. Os alunos classificarão os adjetivos e expressões em positivos e negativos para em seguida usá-los nas respostas às primeiras perguntas. Essa atividade será usada para contextualização. O *Listening* introduz as *if-clauses*. Peça aos alunos que ouçam a primeira estrofe e retirem dois exemplos de sentenças condicionais. Eles devem sublinhar o verbo da *if-clause* e dizer qual é o tempo verbal utilizado (tipo 2 – *would+verb+ if+simple past*). Depois disso, devem ouvir a segunda estrofe e reescrevê-la de uma forma positiva. Faça o primeiro verso como modelo. Chame a atenção para o uso da palavra *even* que enfatiza o significado de que tudo ficará bem, *mesmo* que algo negativo aconteça. Durante o *After listening* os alunos vão relacionar as expressões de acordo com o contexto e finalmente completar as sentenças usando o condicional.

Answer key

Before listening

1.

Positive meaning	Negative meaning
cheerful, happy, fortunate, lucky, pleased, walking on air, on cloud nine, flying high.	miserable, heartbroken, down, hopeless, pathetic, depressed, unhappy, sorry.

2. Open answer.

Listening

1. I would be good even if I did nothing
   I would be good even if I got the thumbs down
   I would be good if I got and stayed sick
   I would be good even if I gained ten pounds

2. I would be good even if I did nothing
   I would be good even if I got the thumbs down
   I would be good if I got and stayed sick
   I would be good even if I gained ten pounds

   The verbs are in the simple past.

3. Open answers. Suggestions:
   That I would be fine if I earned a lot of money.
   That I would be good if my hair grew long.
   That I would be great if I was a queen.
   That I would be grand if I was wise.

After listening

1.   (d) I was rejected.
    (a) I feel indifferent.
    (b) I was very angry.
    (c) I was holding tight.

2.   Open answers.

Lyrics

"That I would be good"

That I would be good even if I did nothing
That I would be good even if I got the thumbs down
That I would be good if I got and stayed sick
That I would be good even if I gained ten pounds

That I would be fine even if I went bankrupt
That I would be good if I lost my hair and my youth
That I would be great if I was no longer queen
That I would be grand if I was not all knowing

That I would be loved even when I numb myself
That I would be good even when I am overwhelmed
That I would be loved even when I was fuming
That I would be good even if I was clinging

That I would be good even if I lost sanity
That I would be good whether with or without you

Colors of the wind

Disney

INFORMAÇÕES TÉCNICAS

Composição: Alan Menken
Estilo: Balada
Cantor: Judy Kuhn na voz de Pocahontas
Tema: Natureza e diversidade cultural

Informações sobre a música

"Colors of the wind" ganhou o Oscar de Melhor Canção Original do filme de animação *Pocahontas*, da Disney. Ela também ganhou o Globo de Ouro na mesma categoria, bem como o Prêmio Grammy de melhor canção escrita para um filme. A canção apresenta um ponto de vista de que a Terra é uma entidade viva onde a humanidade está ligada a tudo na natureza. Na canção, Pocahontas está conversando com John Smith, incentivando-o a não pensar na natureza como algo que ele possa conquistar ou possuir, mas sim como constituída de seres para respeitar e conviver em harmonia. A canção também fala sobre diversidade cultural.

Teaching tips

Contextualize com os alunos, perguntando se eles assistiram ao filme *Pocahontas*. Pergunte a eles qual o tema principal do filme e se eles conhecem algum outro filme que aborda o mesmo tema. Eles devem responder às perguntas do *Before listening* em dupla. Leia com eles as perguntas do *Listening* antes de colocar a música. Na primeira questão eles devem ouvir as primeiras quatro estrofes e dar um título adequado para cada uma. Toque uma estrofe por vez e envolva a classe toda na atividade. Peça aos alunos que discutam qual seria o melhor título para aquela estrofe. Na segunda questão eles vão ouvir a música e prestar atenção a duas perguntas que Pocahontas faz a John Smith. Na terceira, as sentenças devem ser completadas de acordo com a música e na quarta eles deverão retirar da música o verso onde Pocahontas diz que todos nós estamos interconectados. Os alunos devem fazer as questões do *After listening* em duplas, elaborando uma lista de ações que eles podem fazer para ajudar a natureza e, em seguida, ler a estrofe e interpretá-la. Como *homework* você pode pedir que assistam ao filme em inglês e que tragam mais informações sobre o tema para a aula seguinte.

Answer key

Before listening

1. Open answers.

2. Open answers.

3. Open answers.

4. Open answers.

5. Open answers.

6. Suggested answer: People have different cultures and believe in different things. We usually think that people who think and look like us are the ones who are correct. Only when we live in different cultures can we understand and learn different points of view.

7. Open answer.

Listening

1. Suggested answers:
    1a.: Who is the savage?
    2a: The earth is a living being
    3a.: Learn from strangers
    4a.: Can you connect to nature?

2. Have you ever heard the wolf cry to the blue corn moon? Or ask the grinning bobcat why he grinned?

3. a) Can you sing with all the voices of the mountain?
    b) Can you paint with all the colors of the wind?

4. And we are all connected to each other
    In a circle in a hoop that never ends.

After listening

1. Open answer.

2. Open answer.

Lyrics

"Colors of the wind"

You think I'm an ignorant savage
And you've been so many places, I guess it must be so
But still I cannot see, if the savage one is me
How can there be so much that you don't know?
You don't know...
You think you own whatever land you land on
The earth is just a dead thing you can claim
But I know every rock and tree and creature

Has a life, has a spirit, has a name
You think the only people who are people
Are the people who look and think like you
But if you walk the footsteps of a stranger
You'll learn things you never knew you never knew
Have you ever heard the wolf cry to the blue corn moon
Or ask the grinning bobcat why he grinned
Can you sing with all the voices of the mountain
Can you paint with all the colors of the wind
Can you paint with all the colors of the wind
Come run the hidden pine trails of the forest
Come taste the sun-sweet berries of the earth
Come roll in all the riches all around you
And for once never wonder what they're worth
The rainstorm and the river are my brothers
The heron and the otter are my friends
And we are all connected to each other
In a circle in a hoop that never ends
How high does that sycamore grow
If you cut it down then you'll never know
And you'll never hear the wolf cry to the blue corn moon
For whether we are white or copper skinned
We need sing with all the voices of the mountain
We need paint with all the colors of the wind
You can own the earth and still
All you'll own is earth until
You can paint with all the colors of the wind

The living years

Mike And The Mechanics

INFORMAÇÕES TÉCNICAS

Composição: Mike Rutherford and B. A. Robertson
Estilo: Rock
Integrantes: Mike Rutherford, Paul Carrack (and Paul Young), Adrian Lee and Peter Van Hooke.
Site oficial: http://www.houseofmanyrooms.com/
Tema: Conflito entre gerações

Informações sobre a banda e música

Mike & The Mechanics é um banda inglesa de pop rock formada em 1985 como um projeto paralelo de Mike Rutherford — um dos membros fundadores do Genesis — que se tornou um sucesso. "The living years" foi lançada em 1989 no álbum do mesmo nome. Escrita por B. A. Robertson, a música é sobre fatos reais. B. A. havia perdido seu pai e lamentava a falta de comunicação entre os dois. Nessa mesma época, B. A. teve seu primeiro filho. "The living years" ganhou muitos prêmios e, apesar de ter sido lançada em 1989, continua sendo muito ouvida.

Teaching tips

Organize a classe em duplas. Durante o *Before listening* os alunos terão oportunidade de discutir suas opiniões a respeito de conflitos de gerações. Os alunos respondem à primeira atividade individualmente e depois comparam suas respostas com seus parceiros. Dependendo da faixa etária de seu grupo, é interessante acrescentar informações sobre as gerações X e Y através de leitura. Há uma grande discussão a respeito desse assunto na internet, principalmente quando se trata de recrutamento. Se houver tempo, abra a discussão com a classe toda. Durante o *Listening*, os alunos fazem as atividades de *listening* e *writing* individualmente e depois comparam com seus pares. O *After listening* pode ser feito individualmente ou em dupla. Reforce o reconhecimento do *simple past* e a produção de sentenças usando esse tempo verbal e também *I wish I could have...*

Answer key

Before listening

1. Open answers.

Listening

1. Open answer.

2. Open answer. Suggestion:
   His father died before he could have talked to him about important issues.
   "I just wish I could have told him in the living years."

3. *Say it loud, say it clear*
   You can listen as well as you hear
   It's too late when we die
   To admit we don't see eye to eye.

4.

NEGATIVE	POSITIVE
blames, frustrations, prisoner, hostage, fears, imperfect, afraid, tears	hopes, perfect, agreement

After listening

1. *I <u>wasn't</u> there that morning*
   When my father <u>passed</u> away
   I <u>didn't get</u> to tell him
   All the things I <u>had</u> to say.
   I think I <u>caught</u> his spirit
   Later that same year
   I'm sure I <u>heard</u> his echo
   In my baby's new born tears
   I just wish I <u>could</u> have told him
   In the living years.

2. Open answers.

Lyrics

"The living years"

Every generation
Blames the one before
And all of their frustrations
Come beating on your door
I know that I'm a prisoner
To all my father held so dear
I know that I'm a hostage
To all his hopes and fears
I just wish I could have told him
In the living years
Crumpled bits of paper
Filled with imperfect thoughts
Stilted conversations
I'm afraid that's all we've got
You say you just don't see it
He says it's perfect sense
You just can't get agreement

In this present tense
We all talk a different language
Talking in defense
Say it loud, say it clear
You can listen as well as you hear
It's too late when we die
To admit we don't see eye to eye
So we open up a quarrel
Between the present and the past
We only sacrifice the future
It's the bitterness that lasts
So don't yield to the fortunes
You sometimes see as fate
It may have a new perspective
On a different day
And if you don't give up,
And don't give in
You may just be OK
I wasn't there that morning
When my father passed away
I didn't get to tell him
All the things I had to say.
I think I caught his spirit
Later that same year
I'm sure I heard his echo
In my baby's new born tears
I just wish I could have told him
In the living years

Vienna

Billy Joel

INFORMAÇÕES TÉCNICAS

Composição: Billy Joel
Estilo: Soft rock
Cantor: Billy Joel
Site oficial: http://www.billyjoel.com/
Tema: O uso do tempo

Informações sobre o cantor e a música

William Martin Joel nasceu no Bronx, em New York, em 1949. É pianista, compositor e cantor. "Vienna" pertence ao álbum *The stranger* e foi inspirada em uma viagem feita por ele a Viena, Áustria, para encontrar seu pai. Ele não via o pai desde os oito anos.

Teaching tips

Organize a classe em duplas e faça a primeira atividade do *Before listening* para introduzir o tema e contextualizá-lo. Peça aos alunos que comparem as respostas e descubram qual deles é o mais ansioso. A terceira e a quarta atividade trabalham expressões e seus significados. É importante que os alunos construam sentenças com as expressões para fixar o significado das mesmas. Durante o *Listening* os alunos vão ouvir toda a música, buscando versos que tenham o mesmo sentido das sentenças dadas. Leia as sentenças com eles antes de ouvir a música. Na segunda atividade, os alunos devem completar os versos e em seguida discutir com seu par o significado da estrofe toda. Eles devem concordar ou discordar do que foi colocado pelo autor. Durante o *After listening* os alunos, em pares, vão criar um título para a estrofe apresentada. É interessante abrir essa questão com a classe toda, pois os títulos podem variar bastante. A segunda atividade aborda os marcadores de oposição *(contrasting)* – *"but"*, *"although"* e *"though"*. Se for oportuno, faça uma revisão desses *discourse markers* – além de *contrasting, linking ("in addition", "moreover")* e *consequence ("therefore", "as a result")*. A última atividade resume o significado da música toda para cada uma das duplas. Abra a discussão para toda classe em seguida.

Answer key

Before listening

1.   Open answers.

2.   Open answers.

3.   (b)   settle down = cool it off
     (e)   embark on = kick it off
     (d)   gain ground = get ahead of yourself
     (a)   diminish = slow down
     (c)   break down = burn it down

4.   Open answers.

Listening

1.   a)   You're so ahead of yourself that you forgot what you need.
     b)   But then if you're so smart, tell me why are you still so afraid?
     c)   You got so much to do and only so many hours in a day.
     d)   You can't be everything you wanna be before your time.

2.   *You've got your passion. You've got your pride,*
     But don't you know that only fools are satisfied?
     Dream on, but don't imagine they'll all come true.
     When will you realize? Vienna waits for you.

3. Open answer.

After listening

1. Open answer. Suggestion:
   Take it easy.

2. Dream on, but don't imagine they'll all come true.
   a) <u>But</u> then if you're so smart, tell me why are you still so afraid?
   b) You can't be everything you wanna be before your time, / <u>Although</u> it's so romantic on the borderline tonight
   c) Too bad, <u>but</u> it's the life you lead.
   d) <u>Though</u> you can see when you're wrong, / You know, you can't always see when you're right, you're right.
   e) You've got your pride, / <u>But</u> don't you know that only fools are satisfied?

3. Open answer.

Lyrics

"Vienna"

Slow down, you crazy child.
You're so ambitious for a juvenile.
But then if you're so smart, tell me why are you still so afraid?
Where's the fire? What's the hurry about?
You better cool it off before you burn it out.
You got so much to do and only so many hours in a day.

Don't you know that when the truth is told
That you can get what you want or you can just get old?
You're gonna kick off before you even get halfway through.
When will you realize? Vienna waits for you.

Slow down, you're doing fine.
You can't be everything you wanna be before your time,
Although it's so romantic on the borderline tonight, tonight.
Too bad, but it's the life you lead.
You're so ahead of yourself that you forgot what you need.
Though you can see when you're wrong,
You know, you can't always see when you're right, you're right.

You've got your passion. You've got your pride,
But don't you know that only fools are satisfied?
Dream on, but don't imagine they'll all come true.
When will you realize? Vienna waits for you.

Slow down, you crazy child.
Take the phone off the hook and disappear for a while.
It's all right you can afford to lose a day or two.
When will you realize? Vienna waits for you.

Don't you know that when the truth is told
That you can get what you want or you can just get old?
You're gonna kick off before you even get halfway through.
Why don't you realize? Vienna waits for you.
When will you realize? Vienna waits for you.

Informações técnicas, *Teaching tips, Answer keys e Lyrics*

Vinte atividades fotocopiáveis de 50 minutos

Wonderful tonight

Eric Clapton

INFORMAÇÕES TÉCNICAS

Composição: Eric Clapton
Estilo: Rock
Cantor: Eric Clapton
Site oficial: http://www.ericclapton.com/
Tema: Amor

Informações sobre o cantor e música

"Wonderful tonight" é uma música escrita por Eric Clapton. Foi incluída no álbum *Slowhand*, de 1977. Clapton escreveu essa música sobre Pattie Boyd, que menciona o fato em sua autobiografia *Wonderful tonight: George Harrison, Eric Clapton and me*.

No dia 7 de setembro, Clapton escreveu essa música enquanto esperava Boyd se arrumar para irem a festa de Paul e Linda McCartney.

Essa música aparece no comercial SBC em 2005 e também no final da sexta temporada de *Friends*, depois que Chandler pede Mônica em casamento.

Teaching tips

Organize a classe em duplas. Pergunte aos alunos se eles gostam de sair com os amigos e quem eles acham que demora mais tempo para se arrumar: homens ou mulheres. Se possível faça essas perguntas em inglês. Eles devem completar a tabela da primeira questão e escrever o que as mulheres e os homens fazem antes de sair. Durante a audição da música eles devem identificar as três ações que Eric Clapton descreve. Peça a eles que identifiquem também a pergunta que a mulher fez ao parceiro. Em duplas, os alunos devem pensar em outras três perguntas que as mulheres normalmente fazem aos homens.

Revise a ordem dos adjetivos com os alunos e peça a eles que identifiquem na música como Eric Clapton descreve o cabelo de sua esposa. Eles devem ler as palavras na atividade 4 para colocá-las na ordem correta. Por último, peça a eles que ouçam a música e identifiquem as rimas.

Durante o *After listening* os alunos podem descrever seus amigos usando a ordem correta dos adjetivos.

Answer key

Before listening

1. Suggestions:

What boys do before they go out to a party	What girls do before they go out to a party
Have a shower Choose their clothes Have something to eat Go out	Choose their clothes Have a shower Dry their hair Put on their make up Change their clothes Try on many other clothes Choose their shoes Call their friends

Listening

1. She wonders what clothes to wear, puts on her make-up and brushes her hair.

2. Do I look all right?
   Do my shoes match?
   Does my hair look all right?
   Does this dress look good?
   Do you like this perfurm?

3. long blonde hair
    bright blue eyes
    short black hair
    beautiful green eyes
    big red nose
    long black eye lashes

4. wear – hair
    right – tonight
    see – me
    right – tonight
    eyes – realize
    head – bed

After listening

1. Open answer.

Lyrics

"Wonderful tonight"

It's late in the evening; she's wondering what clothes to wear.
She puts on her make-up and brushes her long blonde hair.
And then she asks me, "Do I look all right?"
And I say, "Yes, you look wonderful tonight."
We go to a party and everyone turns to see
This beautiful lady that's walking around with me.
And then she asks me, "Do you feel all right?"
And I say, "Yes, I feel wonderful tonight."

I feel wonderful because I see
The love light in your eyes.

And the wonder of it all
Is that you just don't realize how much I love you.
It's time to go home now and I've got an aching head,
So I give her the car keys and she helps me to bed.

And then I tell her, as I turn out the light,
I say, "My darling, you were wonderful tonight.
Oh my darling, you were wonderful tonight."

With my own two hands

Ben Harper

INFORMAÇÕES TÉCNICAS

Composição: Ben Harper

Estilo: Soul, reggae

Cantores: Ben Harper / Bem Harper e Jack Johnson

Site oficial: http://www.benharper.com/

Tema: Fazer um mundo melhor.

Informações sobre o cantor e a música

Nascido em Los Angeles em 1969, Benjamin Chase Harper cresceu ouvindo blues, soul, R&B e reggae. Essa música faz parte do álbum *Diamonds on the inside*" e tem como foco o que nós como indivíduos podemos fazer para mudar o mundo para melhor. Ben Harper a escreveu em 2003 e ganhou prêmios importantes naquele ano na Europa. Uma outra versão da música, cantada por Jack Johnson, faz parte da trilha sonora do filme infantil *Curious George*.

Teaching tips

Inicie a aula colocando o título da música na lousa e mostrando os dois primeiros minutos do primeiro vídeo sem som. Oriente os alunos a refletir sobre as imagens e deduzir qual é o tema da letra da música. Em seguida mostre os mesmos dois minutos com som e peça aos alunos que conversem em duplas e confirmem se suas hipóteses são verdadeiras. Passe para a terceira e quarta pergunta que eles devem responder individualmente. Coloque algumas respostas na lousa. Durante o *Listening*, mostre o vídeo de Ben Harper cantando e oriente para que façam a primeira e a segunda atividade. Observe que existem algumas sentenças onde o modal *can* está implícito. Reforce o uso do modal *can* com o sentido de *ser capaz* e a forma do comparativo. Ouçam novamente para continuar as atividades em duplas. Durante o *After listening* peça aos alunos que façam a primeira atividade em dupla. Em seguida coloque alguns exemplos dos alunos na lousa. Mostre o terceiro vídeo com a versão em dueto de Jack Johnson e Ben Harper para que os alunos falem a respeito de suas preferências e justifiquem usando a sentença: *I prefer... because...*

Answer key

Before listening

1. Open answer.

2. Watch the video clip again (with sound) and confirm your hypothesis.

3. Open answer.

4. Open answer. Suggestions:
   I can save energy.
   I can save water.
   I can use my bike.
   I can avoid polluting.
   I can reuse plastic.

Listening

1. a) I can change the world.
   b) I can make peace on Earth.
   c) I can clean up the earth.
   d) I can reach out to you.
   e) I can hold you.
   f) I can comfort you.

2. a) better
   a) kinder
   b) brighter
   c) safer

After listening

1. Open answer.

2. Open answer.

Lyrics

"With my own two hands"

I can change the world
With my own two hands
Make it a better place
With my own two hands
Make it a kinder place
With my own two hands
With my own, with my own two hands
I can make peace on earth
With my own two hands
I can clean up the earth
With my own two hands
I can reach out to you
With my own two hands
With my own, with my own two hands
I'm gonna make it a brighter place
With my own two hands
I'm gonna make it a safer place
With my own two hands
I'm gonna help human race
With my own two hands

With my own, with my own two hands
With my own, with my own two hands
I can hold you
In my own two hands
I can comfort you
With my own two hands
But you've got to use
Use your own two hands
Use your own, use your own two hands
Use your own, use your own two hands
With our own
With our own two hands
With our own
With our own two hands
Oh, you got to use your own two hands
With our own, with our own two hands
With our own, with our own two hands
With our own, with our own two hands

I believe I can fly

R. Kelly

INFORMAÇÕES TÉCNICAS

Composição: R. Kelly
Estilo: Soul
Cantor: R. Kelly
Site oficial: http://www.r-kelly.com/
Tema: Autoconfiança, autoestima

Informações sobre o cantor e música

Robert Sylvester Kelly nasceu em Chicago. R. Kelly, seu nome artístico, é conhecido como o rei do R&B (rythm and blues). A música "I believe I can fly" foi lançada em 1996. Composta e cantada por R. Kelly, foi trilha sonora do filme *Space Jam* com Michael Jordan e o elenco do Looney Tunes. Em 2011, R. Kelly cantou em dueto com a vencedora do X Factor Melanie Amaro. Em 2012, o elenco de *Glee* cantou a música no episódio 14 ("On my way") da terceira temporada.

Teaching tips

Existem três versões desta música em vídeo. Sugerimos que a versão original cantada por R. Kelly seja usada para fazer as primeiras atividades. Durante o *Before listening* peça aos alunos que levantem hipóteses a respeito do título da música em pares. Reforce o significado da palavra *believe* e do modal *can*. Mostre os dois primeiros minutos do vídeo com som e peça aos alunos que confirmem suas hipóteses baseando-se nas imagens e na letra da música. É uma boa oportunidade para introduzir a expressão "spread my wings". Tente usar a língua-alvo fazendo mímica. Dependendo do nível de seu grupo, use a língua-alvo o tempo todo. Em seguida, mostre o vídeo novamente e peça aos alunos que organizem os versos da primeira estrofe. Mostre novamente para que completem o refrão. Depois eles devem comparar as respostas com seus pares. A terceira questão do *Listening* é para explicar o significado da sentença e encontrar uma justificativa na letra da música. Na última eles devem responder verdadeiro ou falso e justificar com um verso da música. Durante o *After listening*, mostre as duas outras versões da música. A primeira sugerida é o dueto de R. Kelly com Melanie Amaro, vencedora do programa X Factor. A segunda é a versão apresentada pelos cantores do seriado *Glee*. O objetivo é ouvir a música mais vezes para tentar cantá-la. Leve os alunos a opinar a respeito da versão que mais lhes agradou.

Answer key

Before listening

1. Open answer. Suggestion:
   It's about somebody who feels ready to do something he thought he wasn't able to do before.

2. Open answer. Suggestion:
   You can see the singer spreading his arms as if he could fly.

Listening

1. (2) And life was nothing but an awful song
   (4)   I'm leaning on the everlasting arms
   (5) If I can see it, then I can do it
   (1) I used to think that I could not go on
   (3) But now I know the meaning of true love
   (6) If I just believe it, there's nothing to it

2. I believe I can fly
   I believe I can touch the <u>sky</u>
   I think about it every <u>night</u> and <u>day</u>
   Spread my wings and fly <u>away</u>

I believe I can soar
I see me running through that <u>open door</u>
I believe I can fly.

3. Open answer. Suggestion:
    He means he can do everything he wants to do.
    He means you are able to do anything you want if you believe it.
    He says he knows the meaning of true love now.

4. (F) Life was easy for him. And life was nothing but an awful song.
    (T) He has found his love. But now I know the meaning of true love.
    (T) He thinks life begins inside of him. But first I know it starts inside of me, oh.
    (T) He was having a nervous breakdown. See I was on the verge of breaking down.

After listening

1. http://www.youtube.com/watch?v=o7oDz4omME4
    (duet with Melanie Amaro, winner of the X Factor 2011)

    http://www.youtube.com/watch?v=qKPS1ueL_vE
    (Glee cast)

2. Open answer.

Lyrics

"I believe I can fly"

I used to think that I could not go on
And life was nothing but an awful song
But now I know the meaning of true love
I'm leaning on the everlasting arms

If I can see it, then I can do it
If I just believe it, there's nothing to it

I believe I can fly
I believe I can touch the sky
I think about it every night and day
Spread my wings and fly away
I believe I can soar
I see me running through that open door
I believe I can fly
I believe I can fly
I believe I can fly

See I was on the verge of breaking down
Sometimes silence can seem so loud
There are miracles in life I must achieve
But first I know it starts inside of me, oh

If I can see it, then I can be it
If I just believe it, there's nothing to it

I believe I can fly
I believe I can touch the sky
I think about it every night and day
Spread my wings and fly away
I believe I can soar
I see me running through that open door
I believe I can fly
I believe I can fly
I believe I can fly

Hey, 'cause I believe in me, oh

If I can see it, then I can do it
If I just believe it, there's nothing to it

I believe I can fly
I believe I can touch the sky

I think about it every night and day
Spread my wings and fly away
I believe I can soar
I see me running through that open door
I believe I can fly
I believe I can fly
I believe I can fly

Hey, if I just spread my wings
I can fly
I can fly
I can fly, hey, If I just spread my wings, I can fly, Fly-eye-eye

Born this way

Lady Gaga

INFORMAÇÕES TÉCNICAS

Composição: Lady Gaga
Estilo: Pop
Cantora: Lady Gaga
Site oficial: www.ladygaga.com.br
Tema: Diversidade racial, sexual, preconceito

Informações sobre a cantora e a música

Cantora, compositora e produtora musical americana, Lady Gaga disse: "*Born this way* será o hino da nossa geração. Ela é a melhor música que eu já escrevi". Essa música pertence ao álbum de mesmo nome e foi lançado em 2011. Ela vendeu mais de 1 milhão de cópias em apenas cinco dias.

Teaching tips

A letra de "Born this way" é polêmica e trata de sexualidade, diversidade racial e preconceito. A atividade a ser desenvolvida deve ser adequada à faixa etária de seu grupo e pode ser utilizada para rever ou reforçar a aprendizagem do imperativo em inglês nas formas afirmativa e negativa.

Organize a classe em duplas para que reflitam sobre o título da música. Os alunos devem levantar hipóteses sobre o tema da canção. Dependendo do nível do grupo, a atividade pode ser feita em inglês ou na língua materna. Em seguida os alunos leem os versos e confirmam (ou não) suas hipóteses. As palavras da questão 3 são todas relacionadas ao tema. Algumas são cognatas de fácil entendimento e outras (como *prejudice* – preconceito, *bullying* – intimidação) podem ser explicadas, comentadas e até mesmo traduzidas. O objetivo da questão é contextualizar. Na primeira questão do *Listening*, os alunos precisam completar as sentenças antes de ouvir a música para que tenham oportunidade de ler e deduzir seus significados. Em seguida os alunos ouvem a música com mais objetividade. Toque a música novamente e peça que verifiquem as respostas em pares. Na questão 2 os alunos devem ouvir a música e encontrar as palavras que rimam.

Durante o *After listening* peça a eles que leiam as sentenças individualmente e verifiquem que tempo verbal foi utilizado e como formamos o imperativo afirmativo e negativo. Essas atividades também podem ser feitas como *homework*.

Answer key

Before listening

1. Open answer. Suggestion:
    The lyrics can be about physical characteristics, sexuality, prejudice etc.

2. Open answer. Suggestion:
    The lyrics are about respecting yourself and being respected.

3. Open answer but all the words can be related to the lyrics of the song.

Listening

1. a) *So hold your head up, girl and you'll go far, listen to me when I say*
        Don't hide yourself in regret, just love yourself and you're set
        Don't be a drag, just be a queen
        Rejoice and love yourself today
        Give yourself prudence and love your friends

    b) Listen to the song to check your work.

2. youth: truth
    far: are

way: say
regret: set

After listening

1. a) Imperative.
   b) To give orders, strong suggestions.

2. Complete the sentences.
   a) To form the imperative affirmative we use <u>the base form</u> of the verb.
   b) To form the imperative negative we use <u>don't</u> + <u>the base form</u> of the verb.

3. Open answers. Suggestions:
   a) Don't judge people for their appearance.
   b) Be open-minded. Accept differences.

4. Open answer.

Lyrics

"Born this way"

It doesn't matter if you love him, or capital H-I-M
Just put your paws up
'Cause you were born this way, baby

My mama told me when I was young
We are all born superstars
She rolled my hair and put my lipstick on
In the glass of her boudoir

"There's nothin' wrong with lovin' who you are"
She said, "'cause he made you perfect, babe"
"So hold your head up, girl and you'll go far
Listen to me when I say"

I'm beautiful in my way
'Cause God makes no mistakes
I'm on the right track, baby
I was born this way

Don't hide yourself in regret
Just love yourself and you're set
I'm on the right track, baby
I was born this way

Ooo, there ain't no other way
Baby, I was born this way
Baby, I was born this way

Ooo, there ain't no other way
Baby, I was born this way
I'm on the right track, baby
I was born this way

Don't be a drag, just be a queen
Don't be a drag, just be a queen
Don't be a drag, just be a queen
Don't be!

Give yourself prudence
And love your friends
Subway kid, rejoice your truth

In the religion of the insecure
I must be myself, respect my youth

A different lover is not a sin
Believe capital H-I-M (hey, hey, hey)
I love my life, I love this record and
Mi amore vole fe yah (love needs faith)

I'm beautiful in my way
'Cause God makes no mistakes
I'm on the right track, baby
I was born this way

Don't hide yourself in regret
Just love yourself and you're set
I'm on the right track, baby
I was born this way

Ooo, there ain't no other way
Baby, I was born this way
Baby, I was born this way

Ooo, there ain't no other way
Baby, I was born this way
I'm on the right track, baby
I was born this way

Don't be a drag, just be a queen
Whether you're broke or evergreen
You're black, white, beige, chola descent
You're Lebanese, you're orient
Whether life's disabilities
Left you outcast, bullied or teased
Rejoice and love yourself today
'Cause baby, you were born this way

No matter gay, straight or bi
Lesbian, transgendered life
I'm on the right track, baby
I was born to survive
No matter black, white or beige
Chola or orient made
I'm on the right track, baby
I was born to be brave

I'm beautiful in my way
'Cause God makes no mistakes
I'm on the right track, baby
I was born this way

Don't hide yourself in regret
Just love yourself and you're set
I'm on the right track, baby
I was born this way

Ooo, there ain't no other way
Baby, I was born this way
Baby, I was born this way

Ooo, there ain't no other way
Baby, I was born this way
I'm on the right track, baby
I was born this way

I was born this way, hey!
I was born this way, hey!
I'm on the right track, baby
I was born this way, hey!

A day in the life

The Beatles

INFORMAÇÕES TÉCNICAS

Composição: John Lennon e Paul McCartney
Estilo: Pop
Integrantes: John Lennon, Paulo McCartney, Ringo Starr, George Harrison
Site oficial: www.thebeatles.com
Tema: Rotinas

Informações sobre a banda e a música

"A day in the life" é uma canção dos Beatles lançada no álbum *Sgt. Pepper's Lonely Hearts Club Band*, de 1967. Essa música foi o resultado da junção de duas músicas distintas: uma composta por John Lennon e a outra por Paul McCartney.

Teaching tips

Introduza o tópico usando as perguntas do *Before listening*. Se sua classe for de nível muito básico, as perguntas podem ser feitas na língua materna mas as respostas devem ser na língua-alvo. Na primeira atividade do *Listening* peça aos alunos que ouçam a música e prestem atenção nos verbos usados no tempo passado. Eles devem preencher a tabela com os verbos. Na segunda atividade eles vão usar esses verbos para falar sobre suas próprias atividades no passado. Peça a eles que escrevam um parágrafo usando o máximo de verbos possível. Na atividade 3 eles devem ler as palavras e escrever outras de sentido oposto.

Na primeira atividade do *After listening* peça aos alunos que descrevam um dia de rotina da semana anterior. Enfatize o uso do tempo passado. A segunda atividade é uma pesquisa na net sobre outra música que fale sobre rotina. Eles devem ler a letra da música e avaliar se o contexto é o mesmo.

Answer key

Before listening

1. Suggested answers:
    They wake up, have a shower, have breakfast, go to school/work/ have lunch/ go to gym/ have dinner/ watch TV etc.

2. Open answer.

1. Suggested answers:
    Type of job, working hours, family, age, religious beliefs, hobbies.

Listening

1.

read	made	was	had	saw	blew
didn't notice		stood	stared		turned

2. Open answer

3. happy — sad
    cry — laugh
    after — before
    hate — love
    big — small
    early — late
    downstairs — upstairs

After listening

1. Open answer

2. Open answer

Lyrics

"A day in the life"

I read the news today oh boy
About a lucky man who made the grade
And though the news was rather sad
Well I just had to laugh
I saw the photograph
He blew his mind out in a car
He didn't notice that the lights had changed
A crowd of people stood and stared
They'd seen his face before
Nobody was really sure
If he was from the House of Lords.

I saw a film today oh boy
The English Army had just won the war
A crowd of people turned away
but I just had to look
Having read the book
I'd love to turn you on

Woke up, fell out of bed,
Dragged a comb across my head
Found my way downstairs and drank a cup,
And looking up I noticed I was late.
Found my coat and grabbed my hat
Made the bus in seconds flat
Found my way upstairs and had a smoke,
and Somebody spoke and I went into a dream

I read the news today oh boy
Four thousand holes in Blackburn, Lancashire
And though the holes were rather small
They had to count them all
Now they know how many holes it takes to fill the Albert Hall.
I'd love to turn you on

I am not a girl, not yet a woman

Britney Spears

INFORMAÇÕES TÉCNICAS

Composição: Dido
Estilo: Pop
Cantora: Britney Spears
Site oficial: http://www.britneyspears.com
Tema: Adolescência, transição da adolescência para a vida adulta

Informações sobre a autora e a música

Britney Jean Spears é cantora, compositora, dançarina e atriz norte-americana. Britney já vendeu mais de 100 milhões de álbuns, 90 milhões de singles, e 40 milhões de DVD's, segundo a Jive Records. Britney Spears nasceu em McComb, Mississippi, e cresceu em Kentwood, Louisiana. Filha de Jamie Parnell Spears,um corretor de imóveis, e Lynne Irene Bridges, uma professora primária, tem um irmão mais velho, Bryan, e uma irmã mais nova, a atualmente atriz e cantora Jamie Lynn. "I'm not a girl, not yet a woman" faz parte da trilha sonora do filme *Crossroads*, que teve Britney como protagonista.

Teaching tips

Introduza o tópico através das duas atividades do *Before listening*. Se sua classe for de nível básico, a discussão pode ser feita em português. O objetivo é contextualizar.

Na primeira atividade do *Listening*, os alunos ouvem somente a primeira estrofe. Peça a eles que coloquem os versos em ordem. Se necessário, eles podem ouvir mais de uma vez. Toque a música até o fim para que façam a segunda atividade de completar e em seguida peça que encontrem os antônimos.

Durante o *After listening* os alunos vão completar as sentenças que apareceram na letra da música com sua própria realidade. Como *homework*, peça aos alunos que escrevam um pequeno parágrafo interpretando a letra da música.

Answer key

Before listening

1. Open answers.

2. Open answers.

Listening

1. (2) *But now I know*
    (4) *Feels like I'm caught in the middle*
    (1) *I used to think I had the answers to everything*
    (3) *That life doesn't always go my way*
    (5) *That's when I realize*
    (8) *While I'm in between*
    (6) *I'm not a girl, not yet a woman*
    (9) *I'm not a girl*
    (7) *All I need is time, a moment that is mine*

2. Fill in the blanks

    There is no need to <u>protect</u> me
    It's <u>time</u> that I
    Learn to face up to this on my <u>own</u>
    I've seen so <u>much more</u> than you know now
    So don't <u>tell</u> me to shut my <u>eyes</u>.

3. a) open: shut
    b) boy: girl
    c) questions: answers

d) nothing: everything

e) man: woman

After listening

1. Open answers. Suggestions:

   a) I used to <u>have many friends when I was a teenager.</u>
   b) It feels like <u>I am going to cry.</u>
   c) Now I realize <u>what you mean</u>.
   d) All I need is <u>love.</u>
   e) There is no need to <u>be afraid of this new phase.</u>

2. Open answer.

Lyrics

"I'm not a girl, not yet a woman"

I used to think I had the answers to everything
But now I know
That life doesn't always go my way
Feels like I'm caught in the middle
That's when I realize

CHORUS

I'm not a girl, not yet a woman
All I need is time, a moment that is mine
While I'm in between
I'm not a girl

There is no need to protect me
It's time that I
Learn to face up to this on my own

I've seen so much more than you know now
So don't tell me to shut my eyes

CHORUS — repeat

But if you look at me closely
You will see it in my eyes
This girl will always find her way

CHORUS

(I'm not a girl) I'm not a girl, don't tell me what to believe
(Not yet a woman) I'm just trying to find the woman in me, yeah
(All I need is time) Oh, all I need is time
(A moment that is mine) That's mine
While I'm in between
I'm not a girl, not yet a woman, not now
All I need is time, a moment that is mine
While I'm in between
I'm not a girl, ooh
Not yet a woman

Secrets

One Republic

INFORMAÇÕES TÉCNICAS

Composição: Ryan Tedder
Estilo: Pop rock
Integrantes: Ryan Tedder, Zach Filkins, Drew Brown, Brent Kutzle, Eddie Fisher
Site oficial: www.onerepublic.net
Tema: Segredos

Informações sobre a banda e a música

One Republic é uma banda pop rock americana formada em 2002. Lançaram seu álbum de estreia, *Dreaming out loud*, em 2007. O primeiro single "Apologize" foi o grande *hit* da banda. "Secrets" é o segundo *single*, parte do álbum *Waking up*.

Teaching tips

Escreva a palavra *secrets* na lousa. Peça que os alunos façam um *brainstorming* da palavra. Eles devem dizer todas as palavras que vêm à mente quando pensam na palavra *secrets*. Em seguida faça as perguntas do *Before listening* e peça aos alunos que respondam em grupo. Leia as perguntas do *Listening* antes de colocar a música para que os alunos a ouçam com objetivos claros.

Na primeira questão eles devem ouvir a música procurando as palavras opostas às da questão. Em seguida, na questão 2, eles devem preencher as lacunas com as palavras que estão abaixo,sem ouvir a música. Eles devem ter coerência. Peça que corrijam ouvindo a música.

Na questão 3 eles vão assinalar verdadeiro ou falso e justificar com um verso da música. Na quarta questão eles devem somente escrever o verso que se refere a uma descrição de um carro.

Durante o *After listening* os alunos vão fazer uma atividade que reforça a ordem dos adjetivos nas sentenças. Em seguida, em duplas, é o momento de responder às perguntas.

Answer key

Before listening

1. Open answers.

Listening

1. interesting: boring
    lies: truth
    put on: take off
    near: far
    small: big
    falls: rises
    high: low

2. *Tell me what you want to hear*
    Something that'll like those ears
    Sick of all the insincere
    So I'm gonna give all my secrets away
    This time
    Don't need another perfect lie
    Don't care if critics never jumped in line
    I'm gonna give all my secrets away

3. (T) He thinks his life is boring. *My life gets kind of boring.*
    (F) He is not going to tell his secrets. *I'm going to tell you everything.*

(F)　He has a big family. *Got no family.*
(T)　He is tired of lying. *Sick of all the insincere.*

4. Whose driver shining big black cars

After listening

1. a)　He has big blue eyes.
   b)　My father has long black hair.
   c)　My friend has a small green car.
   d)　My dog has a big black nose.
   e)　The sky has many pink beautiful clouds.
   f)　The cat has long black whiskers.
   g)　My house has many big blue stain marks on the wall.

2. Open answer.

3. Open answer.

Lyrics

"Secrets"

I need another story
Something to get off my chest
My life gets kind of boring
Need something that I can't confess

Till all my sleeves are stained red
From all the truth that I've said
Come by, it honestly I swear
Thought you saw me wink, no, I've been on the brink, so

[Chorus]
Tell me what you want to hear
Something that'll like those ears
Sick of all the insincere
So I'm gonna give all my secrets away
This time
Don't need another perfect lie
Don't care if critics never jumped in line
I'm gonna give all my secrets away

My God, amazing how we got this far
It's like we were chasing all those stars
Whose driver shining big black cars

And every day I see the news
All the problems that we could solve
And when a situation rises
Just write it into an album
Sitting straight, too low
And I don't really like my flow, oh, so

[Chorus]
Tell me what you want to hear
Something that'll like those ears
Sick of all the insincere
So I'm gonna give all my secrets away
This time
Don't need another perfect lie
Don't care if critics never jump in line
I'm gonna give all my secrets away

Got no reason
Got no shame
Got no family
I can blame
Just don't let me disappear
I'm ma tell you everything

[Chorus 2x]
Tell me what you want to hear
Something that'll like those ears
Sick of all the insincere
So I'm gonna give all my secrets away
This time
Don't need another perfect lie
Don't care if critics never jump in line
I'm gonna give all my secrets away

All my secrets away (x2)

Papa don't preach

Madonna

INFORMAÇÕES TÉCNICAS

Composição: Brian Elliot
Estilo: Eletrônica, Dance, Pop, Pop rock, Tecnopop
Site oficial: www.madonna.com
Tema: Gravidez

Informações sobre a cantora e música

"Papa don't preach" é uma canção escrita por Brian Elliot para o álbum *True blue*, o terceiro de Madonna, lançado em junho de 1986. A letra é a respeito de gravidez na adolescência e aborto.

Teaching tips

Discuta com os alunos as questões do *Before listening*. Peça a eles que falem sobre casos reais e sobre qual seria a postura deles. As questões do *Listening* devem ser lidas antes de ouvir a música. Na primeira questão eles vão ouvir a música e assinalar verdadeiro ou falso. Em seguida os alunos leem a sentença e tentam encontrar um verso com o mesmo sentido na música. Na terceira questão eles vão completar as sentenças de acordo com a música e escrever as palavras que rimam. Em seguida faça as perguntas do *After listening*.

Answer key

Before listening

1. Open answer.

2. Open answer.

3. Open answer.

Listening

1. (F) She is angry at her father.
   (T) She thinks her father is going to be upset.
   (T) She wants her father's advice.
   (T) She loves her boyfriend.
   (F) Her boyfriend does not treat her nicely.
   (F) Her friends tell her not to give up the baby.
   (F) She does not want the baby.
   (T) Her father taught her right from wrong.

2. a) Papa I know you're going to be upset
   b) I maybe young at heart
   c) What I need right now is some good advice, please
   d) But I made up my mind, I'm keeping my baby, oh
   e) I need your help, daddy please be strong

3. a) He <u>says</u> that he's going to <u>marry me</u>
      We can raise a <u>little family</u>
      Maybe we'll be <u>all right</u>
      It's a <u>sacrifice</u>

   b) The rhyming words are: me/ family, right/sacrifice.

After listening

1. Ought to

2. Open answer.

Lyrics

"Papa Don't Preach"

Papa I know you're going to be upset
'Cause I was always your little girl
But you should know by now
I'm not a baby

You always taught me right from wrong
I need your help, daddy please be strong
I maybe young at heart
But I know what I'm saying

The one you warned me all about
The one you said I could do without
We're in an awful mess, and I don't mean maybe — please

Papa don't preach, I'm in trouble deep
Papa don't preach, I've been losing sleep
But I made up my mind, I'm keeping my baby, oh
I'm gonna keep my baby, mmm...

He says that he's going to marry me
We can raise a little family
Maybe we'll be all right
It's a sacrifice

But my friends keep telling me to give it up
Saying I'm too young, I ought to live it up
What I need right now is some good advice, please

Daddy, daddy if you could only see
Just how good he's been treating me
You'd give us your blessing right now
'Cause we are in love, we are in love, so please

Papa don't preach, I'm in trouble deep
Papa don't preach, I've been losing sleep

Oh, I'm gonna keep my baby, ooh
Don't you stop loving me daddy
I know, I'm keeping my baby

Unwritten

Natasha Bedingfield

INFORMAÇÕES TÉCNICAS

Composição: Natasha Bedingfield
Estilo: Pop
Cantora: Natasha Bedingfield
Site oficial: http://www.natashabedingfield.com/global/home
Tema: Maturidade, viver o dia em sua plenitude

Informações sobre a cantora e a música

Natasha Bedingfield é uma cantora e compositora inglesa. Faz muito sucesso nos Estados Unidos, principalmente com a música *Unwritten*. Essa música foi escrita para o irmão da cantora, quando ele completou catorze anos.

Teaching tips

Inicie a aula organizando a classe em duplas, e introduzindo uma discussão sobre a primeira questão do *Before listening*. Antes de passar para a segunda questão explique que essa letra foi escrita por Natasha como presente de aniversário para o irmão de catorze anos. Natasha tenta explicar como se sente um adolescente passando para a vida adulta. Peça aos alunos que façam a segunda e a terceira questão individualmente para em seguida comparar as respostas com seus pares.

Na quarta questão do *Before listening* peça aos alunos que leiam os versos, discutam a mensagem com seus pares e escrevam uma sentença curta a respeito do que foi compreendido. Na última atividade, peça que assistam ao videoclipe sem som e que avaliem se o vídeo representa bem a letra da música. Peça que descrevam algumas cenas. Dependendo do nível de seus alunos essa discussão pode ser feita na língua materna.

O videoclipe será usado para as atividades de *Listening*. Apresente-o aos alunos e peça a eles que tentem complementar as ideias que já tinham a respeito da letra da música. Na segunda questão os alunos vão ouvir a música e escrever as palavras que começam com o prefixo de negação *un-*. Deixe que os alunos deduzam o significado do prefixo. Em seguida apresente outros prefixos de negação usados em inglês. Peça a eles que formem as palavras preenchendo o quadro. Em seguida devem selecionar duas dessas palavras e escrever sentenças com elas.

Answer key

Before listening

1. Open answer.

2. (F) I'm writing a book.
   (T) I'm taking the first steps in my life.
   (T) I'm confused.
   (F) I feel empty.

3. Open answer.
   Suggestion: "Live your life."
   "Release your inhibition, feel the rain on your skin
   No one else can feel it for you, only you can let it in
   No one else, no one else can speak the words on your lips"

4. Open answer. Suggestion:
   We learn when we make mistakes.

5. Open answer.

Listening

1. Open answer.

2. Unwritten, undefined, unplanned, unspoken.

3. It has a negative meaning (not).

After listening

1.

	un-	dis-	i-
important	unimportant		
relevant			irrelavant
able	unable		
successful	unsuccessful		
honest		dishonest	
logical			illogical
order		disorder	

2. Open answers.

Lyrics

"Unwritten"

I am unwritten, can't read my mind, I'm undefined
I'm just beginning, the pen's in my hand, ending
unplanned
Staring at the blank page before you
Open up the dirty window
Let the sun illuminate the words that you could not
find

Reaching for something in the distance
So close you can almost taste it
Release your inhibition
Feel the rain on your skin
No one else can feel it for you
Only you can let it in
No one else, no one else
Can speak the words on your lips
Drench yourself in words unspoken
Live your life with arms wide open
Today is when your book begins
The rest is still unwritten

Oh, oh

I break tradition, sometimes my tries, are outside the
lines
We've been conditioned to not make mistakes, but I
can't live that way

Staring at the blank page before you
Open up the dirty window
Let the sun illuminate the words that you could not
find

Feel the rain on your skin
No one else can feel it for you
Only you can let it in
No one else, no one else
Can speak the words on your lips
Drench yourself in words unspoken
Live your life with arms wide open
Today is when your book begins
The rest is still unwritten

Hallelujah

Leonard Cohen

INFORMAÇÕES TÉCNICAS

Composição: Leonard Cohen
Estilo: Gospel
Cantor: Leonard Cohen
Site oficial: http://www.leonardcohen.com/us/home
Tema: Amor

Informações sobre o cantor e música

Leonard Norman Cohen, cantor, compositor, poeta e escritor canadense, nasceu em Montreal no dia 21 de setembro de 1934. Essa música demonstra como o amor pode ser ao mesmo tempo simples e complicado. Há muitas interpretações diferentes dessa música e definitivamente há referências bíblicas sobre a história do rei Davi. Muitos interpretam que a história do rei Davi é usada para esclarecer o que o cantor realmente sentiu ao compor essa música — como ele se sente traído pelo amor e não acredita mais nele. Esse argumento sobre o amor pode ser comparado com a fé que as pessoas têm em Deus. Quando a vida delas se torna insuportável, as vezes elas também perdem a fé. Outro fator muito importante são as diferentes interpretações da palavra "Hallelujah", que pode ter uma conotação triste, alegre ou de fé.

Teaching tips

Chame a atenção dos alunos para o título da música. Inicie uma discussão sobre o significado que eles conhecem da palavra. Em seguida toque a música uma vez e peça aos alunos que apenas a ouçam para interpretar o sentido que o cantor quis dar à música. É uma atividade de *listening* que deve ser rápida. Não é necessário ouvir toda a música. Não aprofunde muito nesse momento pois os alunos o farão em seguida.

Na atividade seguinte os alunos vão ler as palavras e escrever seus antônimos. Em seguida coloque a música para que eles encontrem as palavras que escreveram. Eles podem bater palma indicando que ouviram a palavra.

Coloque a música mais uma vez, parando em cada verso que termine com a palavra Hallelujah. Peça a os alunos que interpretem a entonação da palavra. Se ela é dita com uma entonação de tristeza, felicidade ou fé.

Na atividade seguinte os alunos vão ordenar as sentenças da estrofe e em seguida prestar atenção ao uso da expressão "I used to...". Eles devem escrever três sentenças de acordo com a realidade de cada um, usando essa estrutura.

Por último toque a música novamente para que façam uma interpretação final. Qual é a mensagem do compositor?

Answer key

Before listening

1. In modern English, "Hallelujah" is frequently spoken to express happiness that a thing hoped or waited for has happened. For most Christians, "Hallelujah" is considered a joyful word of praise to God.

2. Open answer.

3. weak: strong
   fix: break
   after: before
   together: alone
   hot: cold
   fixed: broken
   above: below
   hate: love
   day: night
   worst: best
   everything: nothing
   dark: light

Listening

1. Listen to the song and find the words you wrote in the previous activity.

2. The hallelujah at the end of the first verse is a happy and spiritual one.
    In the second verse, the hallelujah is a very sad and desperate one.
    In the third part, the hallelujah is cold and broken.
    In the forth verse the hallelujah can be interpreted as an excited one.
    In the fifth part this is an uncertain hallelujah, meaning that he is not sure what to believe but he believes anyway.
    In the last part the hallelujah is one of total faith and love for "the Lord".

3. (5) Love is not a victory march
    (1) Baby I have been here before
    (3) I used to live alone before I knew you.
    (6) It's a cold and it's a broken Hallelujah
    (2) I know this room, I've walked this floor
    (4) I've seen your flag on the marble arch

After listening

1. Open answer. Suggestions:
    I used to study French.
    I used to go to school in the afternoon.
    I used to play the piano.

2. Open answer.

Lyrics

"Hallelujah"

I've heard there was a secret chord
That David played, and it pleased the Lord
But you don't really care for music, do you?

It goes like this
The fourth, the fifth
The minor fall, the major lift
The baffled king composing Hallelujah

Hallelujah, Hallelujah
Hallelujah, Hallelujah

Your faith was strong but you needed proof
You saw her bathing on the roof
Her beauty in the moonlight overthrew you
She tied you to a kitchen chair
She broke your throne, and she cut your hair
And from your lips she drew the Hallelujah

Hallelujah, Hallelujah
Hallelujah, Hallelujah

Baby I have been here before
I know this room, I've walked this floor
I used to live alone before I knew you.
I've seen your flag on the marble arch
Love is not a victory march
It's a cold and it's a broken Hallelujah

Hallelujah, Hallelujah
Hallelujah, Hallelujah

There was a time when you let me know
What's really going on below
But now you never show it to me, do you?
And remember when I moved in you
The holy dove was moving too
And every breath we drew was Hallelujah

Hallelujah, Hallelujah
Hallelujah, Hallelujah

Maybe there's a God above
But all I've ever learned from love
Was how to shoot at someone who outdrew you
It's not a cry you can hear at night
It's not somebody who has seen the light
It's a cold and it's a broken Hallelujah

Hallelujah, Hallelujah
Hallelujah, Hallelujah

You say I took the name in vain
I don't even know the name
But if I did, well, really, what's it to you?
There's a blaze of light in every word
It doesn't matter which you heard
The holy or the broken Hallelujah

Hallelujah, Hallelujah
Hallelujah, Hallelujah

I did my best, it wasn't much
I couldn't feel, so I tried to touch
I've told the truth, I didn't come to fool you
And even though it all went wrong
I'll stand before the Lord of Song
With nothing on my tongue but Hallelujah

Hallelujah, Hallelujah
Hallelujah, Hallelujah
Hallelujah, Hallelujah
Hallelujah, Hallelujah
Hallelujah, Hallelujah
Hallelujah, Hallelujah
Hallelujah, Hallelujah
Hallelujah, Hallelujah
Hallelujah

I dreamed a dream

Les Misérables

INFORMAÇÕES TÉCNICAS

Composição: Alain Boublil

Estilo: Romântico

Cantora: Cantado pela personagem Fantine no primeiro ato de *Les Misérables*

Site oficial: http://www.lesmis.com/

Tema: Amor não correspondido

Informações sobre a cantora e a música

"I dreamed a dream" é a canção tema do musical *Os miseráveis*, de 1980, composta por Alain Boublil. *Les Miserables* é um dos musicais mais famosos do mundo. Ela é baseada no romance homônimo de Vitor Hugo. "I dreamed a dream" é um solo cantado por Fantine durante o primeiro ato no musical. A canção é melancólica e calma no início, mas no final a cantora se exalta e a canção demonstra a angústia, a frustração e a insatisfação de Fantine sobre o estado da vida em que ela se encontra. A canção é um lamento.

Teaching tips

Responda às perguntas do *Before listening* com os alunos. Contextualize o assunto e converse sobre os sonhos de cada um. Na atividade de *Listening* leia as sentenças com os alunos antes de colocar a música. Peça a eles que completem com palavras que se encaixem coerentemente. Em seguida os alunos, divididos em duplas, devem comparar com seus pares as palavras que escreveram. Toque a primeira estrofe da música e peça a eles que completem as sentenças com as palavras da música e depois comparem com o que escreveram na atividade anterior. Pergunte aos alunos se eles consideram essa estrofe esperançosa. Eles devem apontar cinco palavras ou sentenças que indicam essa esperança. Em seguida peça aos alunos que observem as palavras que estão na tabela.

Coloque a música novamente para que observem como são usadas essas palavras e seus respectivos prefixos. Explique a eles que esses prefixos são de negação. Após essa atividade os alunos devem completar a coluna da direita usando os prefixos mais apropriados da tabela, e depois corrigir em duplas. Na atividade seguinte eles devem ouvir a próxima estrofe. Pergunte novamente se ela transmite esperança ou não e quais as palavras ou sentenças que indicam isso.

Coloque a música toda para os alunos ouvirem e pergunte qual o tempo verbal predominante na música. Entregue a eles uma cópia da letra para que sublinhem o tempo verbal que citaram. Eles devem estar atentos à última estrofe para avaliar se o sonho dela se realizou. Peça a eles que apontem qual linha da estrofe indica esse fato.

Por último, divida a turma em dois grupos, A e B. Dê as palavras abaixo para o grupo A. Eles devem escolher uma palavra e dizer para o grupo B. Esse grupo deve dizer qual o prefixo de negação mais adequado para essa palavra. Em seguida eles trocam de posição. O grupo B deve dizer a palavra e o grupo A, o prefixo.

rational – proper – responsible – logical – possible – legal – mature – capable – relevant – decent – offensive – personal – regular – respectful – honest – motivated

Answer key

Before listening

1. Open answer.

2. Suggestion: love, peace, no violence, success, desire, happiness, health, family.

3. Compare your notes with other friends and see if you have similar dreams.

Listening

1. Suggestions:
    a) Her hopes were <u>low</u>.
    b) Life was worth <u>taking risks</u>.
    c) Love would never <u>end</u>.
    d) God was <u>angry</u>.
    e) She was <u>happy</u> and not <u>afraid</u>.
    f) All songs were not <u>sung</u>
    g) All wine was not <u>drunk</u>.

2. a) Her hopes were high.
    b) Life was worth <u>living</u>
    c) Love would never <u>die</u>.
    d) God was <u>forgiving</u>.
    e) She was <u>young</u> and not <u>afraid</u>.
    f) All songs were not <u>sung</u>
    g) All wine was not <u>tasted</u>.

3. a) Suggestion:
        Yes, she was hopeful. Her hopes were high, life was worth it, love would
        not die, she was young and not afraid.

    b)

afraid	unafraid
sung	unsung
tasted	untasted

    c)

lucky	unlucky
behave	misbehave
view	review
obey	disobey
healthy	unhealthy
happy	unhappy
possible	impossible

honest	dishonest
legal	illegal
connect	disconnect
cover	uncover
sense	nonsense

4. Suggestion:
    No, she is not hopeful. The tiger comes at night, thunder, tear your heart apart, dream to shame.

5. Simple past

6. Read the lyrics and underline the verb tense you stated in activity 5.

7. No. Her dreams did not come true. *Life has killed the dream I dreamed.*

After listening

1. irrational — improper — irresponsible — illogical — impossible — illegal — immature — incapable — irrelevant — indecent — inoffensive — impersonal — irregular — disrespectful — dishonest — unmotivated

Lyrics

"I dreamed a dream"

I dreamed a dream in time gone by
When hope was high
And life worth living
I dreamed that love would never die
I dreamed that God would be forgiving
Then I was young and unafraid
And dreams were made and used and wasted
There was no ransom to be paid
No song unsung, no wine untasted

But the tigers come at night
With their voices soft as thunder
As they tear your hope apart
As they turn your dream to shame

He slept a summer by my side
He filled my days with endless wonder
He took my childhood in his stride
But he was gone when autumn came

And still I dream he'll come to me
That we will live the years together
But there are dreams that cannot be
And there are storms we cannot weather

I had a dream my life would be
So different from this hell I'm living
So different now from what it seemed
Now life has killed the dream I dreamed.

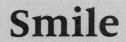

Smile

Uncle Kracker

INFORMAÇÕES TÉCNICAS

Composição: Matthew Shafer (Uncle Kracker)
Estilo: Pop rock
Cantor: Matthew Shafer
Site official: http://www.unclekracker.com/
Tema: Amor

Informações sobre o cantor e a música

Matthew Shafer (nascido em 6 de junho de 1974) é um músico americano conhecido como Uncle Kracker. Seus *singles* mais famosos são "Follow me", "Smile", e "Drift away". Sua música era mais próxima do estilo rap no começo da sua carreira, depois aproximou-se do rock. A música "Smile" faz parte do álbum *Happy hour*.

Teaching tips

Comece a aula fazendo as perguntas do *Before listening*. Coloque a citação na lousa e peça aos alunos que a interpretem. Contextualize o tópico e use exemplos de pessoas famosas. Pergunte aos alunos se eles estão sempre sorrindo ou se são mais sérios.

Em seguida, mostre a primeira atividade para os alunos. Eles devem ler somente a primeira. Toque a primeira estrofe da música e pare. Os alunos deverão fazer a primeira atividade. Em seguida, eles podem ler a segunda e fazer a atividade. Coloque a música e pare após a segunda estrofe. Peça a eles que preencham os espaços. Coloque a música toda para os alunos escutarem e peça que prestem atenção aos comparativos, superlativos e como ele descreve seus sentimentos.

Nas atividades do *After listening* peça aos alunos que escrevam sentenças usando os comparativos e superlativos das palavras do quadro. Em seguida, revise com eles os vários usos da palavra *like*, antes de responderem às perguntas.

Answer key

Before listening

1. Suggestions:
    Thinking about a loved one, listening to a song, seeing happy people, watching children play, looking at beautiful sights, flowers, love notes etc.

2. Suggestion:
    Sometimes you smile because you are happy and have a reason to smile but sometimes you are happy because you smile and your smile brings on good things.

3. Open answer.

Listening

1. Listen to the first stanza. Write the comparative and superlative words you find in the chart below.

COMPARATIVE	SUPERLATIVE
Better Cooler	Best

2. Suggestions:
    I am a better tennis player than she is.
    The weather in São Paulo is cooler than in Rio.
    Agassi is the best tennis player in the world in my opinion.

3. Suggestions:
    a) Smile like you mean it.
    b) You make me sing like a bird.
    c) You make me dance like a freak.
    d) You make me shine like a star.
    e) You make me feel like a monster.
    f) I look like a super star.

4. You make me smile like the sun
   Fall out of bed, sing like a <u>bird</u>
   Dizzy in my head, spin like a <u>record</u>
   Crazy on a Sunday night
   You make me dance like a <u>fool</u>
   Forget how to breathe
   Shine like <u>gold</u>, buzz like a <u>bee</u>
   Just the thought of you can drive me wild.
   Ohh, you make me smile.

After listening

1. Open answers.

2. Open answers.

3. Open answers.

Lyrics

"Smile"

You're better than the best
I'm lucky just to linger in your light
Cooler then the flip side of my pillow, that's right
Completely unaware
Nothing can compare to where you send me,

Lets me know that it's ok, yeah it's ok
And the moments where my good times start to fade

You make me smile like the sun
Fall out of bed, sing like bird
Dizzy in my head, spin like a record
Crazy on a Sunday night
You make me dance like a fool
Forget how to breathe
Shine like gold, buzz like a bee
Just the thought of you can drive me wild
Ohh, you make me smile

Even when you're gone
Somehow you come along
Just like a flower poking the sidewalk crack and just like that
You steal away the rain and just like that

You make me smile like the sun
Fall out of bed, sing like bird
Dizzy in my head, spin like a record
Crazy on a Sunday night
You make me dance like a fool
Forget how to breathe
Shine like gold, buzz like a bee
Just the thought of you can drive me wild
Ohh, you make me smile

Don't know how I lived without you
Cuz everytime that I get around you
I see the best of me inside your eyes
You make me smile
You make me dance like a fool
Forget how to breathe
Shine like gold, buzz like a bee
Just the thought of you can drive me wild

You make me smile like the sun
Fall out of bed, sing like bird
Dizzy in my head, spin like a record
Crazy on a Sunday night
You make me dance like a fool
Forget how to breathe
Shine like gold, buzz like a bee
Just the thought of you can drive me wild
Ohh, you make me smile

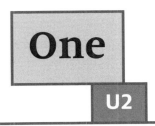

One

U2

INFORMAÇÕES TÉCNICAS

Composição: Bono Vox
Estilo: Rock alternativo, Rock, Pop rock
Integrantes: Bono Vox, The Edge, Adam Clayton e Larry Mullen Jr.
Site oficial: www.u2.com
Tema: Relacionamento

Informações sobre a banda e a música

U2 é uma banda de rock irlandesa formada em 1976, em Dublin. A canção "One" é o terceiro *single* do álbum *Achtung Baby*. Durante a gravação de *Achtung Baby*, surgiram vários conflitos entre a banda, que quase se separou. Nesse momento, o guitarrista The Edge compôs uma progressão de acordes que culminou nessa música. A letra, escrita pelo vocalista Bono, descreve as lutas para manter relações com os outros, mas há várias outras interpretações.

Teaching tips

Coloque a palavra *relationships* na lousa. Pergunte aos alunos o que vem à mente quando escutam essa palavra. Divida a classe em duplas para que respondam às perguntas do *Before listening*.

Na primeira questão do *Listening* peça aos alunos que leiam as sentenças antes de escutar a música. Eles devem numerar as sentenças de acordo com o sentido de cada estrofe. Em seguida é o momento de ouvir a quarta estrofe e interpretar o sentido dos dois versos. Peça a eles que levem em conta o que eles conversaram durante as questões do *Before listening*.

Na terceira questão eles devem ordenar as estrofes e em seguida responder às perguntas. Na questão *d)* eles devem ouvir a música novamente e anotar todas as palavras que rimam. Se houver tempo, eles podem formar sentenças usando essas palavras em outro contexto. Faça as questões do *After listening* com os alunos.

Answer key

Before listening

1. a) Open answer.
    b) Suggestions: mother/child; husband/wife; girlfriend/boyfriend; boss/worker etc
    c) Open answer.
    d) Open answer.
    e) Open answer.
    f) Open answer.

2. a) blame: to hold responsible; find fault with; to place the responsibility for something. Ex: I blame the weather for the accident.

    b) Open answer.

Listening

1. a) (2)
    b) (1)
    c) (3)

2. a) Suggested answer:
    Although they are a couple (one) they have their own feelings, fears and hopes. As a couple they should help each other. They are together but that does not mean they need to think in the same way.

3. a) (4) You ask me to enter, but then you make me crawl
    (1) You say:
    (11) We get to carry each other, carry each other.

(2)   Love is a temple, love a higher law

(10)   One life, but we're not the same.

(5)   And I can't keep holding on to what you got

(7)   One love, one blood

(3)   Love is a temple, love the higher law

(8)   One life you got to do what you should.

(6)   When all you got is hurt.

(9)   One life with each other: sisters, brothers.

(12)   One! One!

b) Suggested answer:
No, I don't think so.
And I can't keep holding on to what you got. When all you got is hurt.

c) Suggested answer:
It can be about a friendship, a parent/child relationship.

d) same/blame; mouth/without; tonight/light; dead/head; forgiveness/Jesus; lot/got; same/again; law/crawl.

After listening

1. Examples: Adam and Eve; Fred and Wilma; Mickey and Minnie; Brad Pitt and Angelina Jolie; Barbie and Ken; Samson and Delilah; Romeo and Juliet; Donald Duck and Daisy etc.

2. Open answer.

Lyrics

"One"

Is it getting better?
Or do you feel the same?
Will it make it easier on you now?

You got someone to blame
You say one love, one life
It's one need in the night
One love, we get to share it
Leaves you, darling, if you don't care for it.
Did I disappoint you?
Or leave a bad taste in your mouth?
You act like you never had love
And you want me to go without
Well, it's too late, tonight,
To drag the past out into the light
We're one, but we're not the same
We get to carry each other, carry each other
One
Have you come here for forgiveness?
Have you come to raise the dead?
Have you come here to play Jesus
to the lepers in your head?
Did I ask too much, more than a lot?
You gave me nothing, now it's all I got
We're one, but we're not the same.
Well, we hurt each other, then we do it again.
You say:
Love is a temple, love a higher law
Love is a temple, love the higher law
You ask me to enter, but then you make me crawl
And I can't keep holding on to what you got
When all you got is hurt.
One love, one blood
One life you got to do what you should.
One life with each other: sisters, brothers.
One life, but we're not the same.
We get to carry each other, carry each other.
One! One!

Goodbye England's rose

Elton John

INFORMAÇÕES TÉCNICAS

Composição: Elton John
Estilo: Pop rock
Cantor: Elton John
Site official: www.eltonjohn.com
Tema: Tributo a alguém

Informações sobre o cantor e a música

Sir Elton Hercules John, (nome de nascença: Reginald Kenneth Dwight) nasceu no dia 25 de março de 1947. Ele é cantor, compositor, pianista e ator inglês. O letrista Bernie Taupin tem sido o compositor de suas músicas desde 1967. Elton John vendeu mais de 250 milhões de discos em sua carreira de quatro décadas.

"Candle in the wind 1997" ou "Goodbye England's rose" é uma reformulação de "Candle in the wind" feita por Elton John e lançada como um *single* de tributo à princesa Diana, Princesa de Gales, que morreu em um acidente de carro em Paris, França. Lançada em setembro de 1997, a canção chegou à primeira posição no Reino Unido, tornando-se o quarto *single* número um de Elton John e vendendo mais de 33 milhões de cópias.

Teaching tips

Analise primeiramente o título com os alunos. Procure saber quais são os cantores ingleses famosos preferidos deles. Eles sabem sobre algum cantor que foi proclamado *"Sir"*? Responda às perguntas do *Before listening* com eles. Na última questão dessa seção, liste na lousa todas as palavras que foram ditas. Coloque a música uma vez para os alunos ouvirem e peça a um aluno que venha à lousa e risque as palavras ditas na letra. Os demais devem ajudar.

Em seguida, os alunos podem escutar a música e completar as sentenças da primeira questão do *Listening*. Pergunte a eles qual sentença é a mais forte no sentido de fazer uma homenagem a alguém. Na questão seguinte os alunos deverão ler as sentenças e relacionar ao verso que contém o contexto da sentença. Eles devem comparar as respostas e justificar a escolha daquele verso.

Durante o *After listening* os alunos vão interpretar a frase *Candle in the wind*. Sugira que pensem em alguma pessoa para a qual eles poderiam fazer uma homenagem e o que eles escreveriam a respeito dessa pessoa.

Answer key

Before listening

1. Open answer.

2. Open answer.

3. Tribute to Martin Luther King, Michael Jackson, Eric Clapton's son, John Lennon, Veterans of World War One, Princess Diana etc.

4. Open answer

Listening

1. a) *The lives were <u>torn apart</u>.*
   b) *You belong to <u>heaven</u>.*
   c) *The stars <u>spell out</u> your name.*
   d) *Like a candle <u>in the wind</u>.*
   e) *These empty days <u>without your smile</u>.*
   f) *Truth brings us <u>to tears</u>.*
   g) *Joy you brought us through the <u>years</u>.*
   h) *From a country lost <u>without your soul</u>.*

2. (c)
You helped people and gave them hope
Goodbye England's rose
May you ever grow in our hearts
You were the grace that placed itself
Where lives were torn apart
You called out to our country
And you whispered to those in pain
Now you belong to heaven
And the stars spell out your name

(b)
You will never be forgotten.
And it seems to me you lived your life
Like a candle in the wind
Never fading with the sunset
When the rain set in
And your footsteps will always fall here
Along England's greenest hills
Your candle's burned out long before
Your legend ever will

(d)
You made us happy with your smile.
Loveliness we've lost
These empty days without your smile
This torch we'll always carry
For our nation's golden child
And even though we try
The truth brings us to tears
All our words cannot express
The joy you brought us through the years

(a)
You were a compassionate person.
Goodbye England's rose
May you ever grow in our hearts
You were the grace that placed itself

Where lives were torn apart
Goodbye England's rose
From a country lost without your soul
Who'll miss the wings of your compassion
More than you'll ever know

After listening

1. Suggestion: A candle in the wind usually burns out, but she will never be forgotten because although the candle burnt out her memories will be forever in every one's heart.

2. Open answer.

Lyrics

"Goodbye England's rose"

Goodbye England's rose
May you ever grow in our hearts
You were the grace that placed itself
Where lives were torn apart
You called out to our country
And you whispered to those in pain
Now you belong to heaven
And the stars spell out your name

[Chorus]
And it seems to me you lived your life
Like a candle in the wind
Never fading with the sunset
When the rain set in
And your footsteps will always fall here
Along England's greenest hills
Your candle's burned out long before

Your legend ever will
Loveliness we've lost
These empty days without your smile
This torch we'll always carry
For our nation's golden child
And even though we try
The truth brings us to tears
All our words cannot express
The joy you brought us through the years

[repeat chorus]
Goodbye England's rose
May you ever grow in our hearts
You were the grace that placed itself
Where lives were torn apart
Goodbye England's rose
From a country lost without your soul
Who'll miss the wings of your compassion
More than you'll ever know

The only exception

Paramore

INFORMAÇÕES TÉCNICAS

Composição: Hayley Williams
Estilo: Rock alternativo, pop rock, punk rock, pop
Integrantes: Hayley Williams, Jeremy Davis e Taylor York
Site oficial: www.paramore.net
Tema: Amor

Informações sobre a banda e a música

Paramore é uma banda americana de rock alternativo, formada em Franklin, Tennessee, no ano de 2004. A banda já lançou três álbuns de estúdio: *All we know is falling*, *Riot!* e *Brand new eyes*. Em 2010 o Paramore sofreu mudanças e os integrantes e irmãos Josh e Zac deixaram a banda. "The only exception" é a canção do terceiro álbum de estúdio: *Brand new eyes*. O videoclip e a música foi lançado em 17 de fevereiro de 2010. Os cantores falam sobre a relação disfuncional dos seus pais, dizendo não acreditar no amor.

Teaching tips

Comece a aula perguntando aos alunos se eles sabem como foi o primeiro encontro dos pais deles, como se conheceram. Pergunte se eles acham que os pais deles são felizes no casamento e faça as perguntas do *Before listening*. Explore esse tema com os alunos e pergunte se eles acreditam em almas gêmeas. Peça aos alunos que leiam as perguntas do *Listening* antes de escutar a música. Na primeira questão, os alunos devem observar o sentimento transmitido pela cantora ao descrever seu pai. Na segunda questão, os alunos devem ler a opinião da cantora sobre a própria mãe. Pergunte aos alunos se eles acham que o relacionamento dos pais influencia nos relacionamentos futuros dos fihos. Depois eles podem responder à terceira questão.

Em seguida os alunos ouvirão a música inteira, prestando atenção nos verbos utilizados pela cantora. Peça a eles que listem os verbos no passado e depois classifiquem-nos como regulares ou irregulares.

Na quinta questão os alunos devem escutar a música novamente e tentar perceber em que estrofe a cantora diz que ela é feliz sozinha. Na sexta e na sétima questão, os alunos devem ordenar a estrofe e buscar o seu sentido. Ela tem um significado positivo ou negativo? Na oitava, eles devem buscar um verso que conforta a cantora. Se necessário, eles podem ler a letra da música.

Nas perguntas do *After listening* o foco está na palavra *exception*. Pergunte aos alunos se aconteceu algo na vida deles que eles possam considerar uma exceção. Em seguida eles irão entender como usar a palavra *exception* em inglês.

Answer key

Before listening

1. Open answer.

2. Open answer.

3. Something to read about wedding traditions:
   <http://www.worldweddingtraditions.com/>
   [Acesso em: 27/07/2012]

   Arranged marriages:
   <http://ezinearticles.com/?The-Reality-of-Arranged-Marriages&id=606>
   [Acesso em: 27/07/2012].

4. Open answer.

5. Open answer.

Listening

1. She saw him cry, his heart was broken and she watched him try to put himself together.

2. Her mother said she would never forget.

3. She said she would never sing of love, unless she thought she really found it. Her parents' relationship made her believe true love was impossible.

4.

Regular verbs in the past	Irregular verbs in the past
watched tried promised lived	broke was swore

5. In the fifth stanza.

6. (4) *I know you're leaving*
   (6) *Leave me with some kind of proof it's not a dream*
   (2) *But I can't*
   (3) *Let go of what's in front of me here*
   (5) *In the morning, when you wake up*
   (1) *I've got a tight grip on reality*

7. Negative. She still thinks he will leave in the morning.

8. You are the only exception.

After listening

1. Open answer

2. Open answers. Suggestion:
   I will only open an exception in case of sickness.
   There are always exceptions to the rule.

Lyrics

"The only exception"

When I was younger
I saw my daddy cry
And curse at the wind
He broke his own heart
And I watched
As he tried to reassemble it

And my momma swore that
She would never let herself forget
And that was the day that I promised
I'd never sing of love
If it does not exist

But darling,
You are the only exception
You are the only exception
You are the only exception
You are the only exception

Maybe I know, somewhere
Deep in my soul
That love never lasts
And we've got to find other ways
To make it alone
Or keep a straight face

And I've always lived like this
Keeping a comfortable, distance
And up until now
I had sworn to myself that I'm content
With loneliness

Because none of it was ever worth the risk
You are the only exception

You are the only exception
You are the only exception
You are the only exception

I've got a tight grip on reality
But I can't
Let go of what's in front of me here
I know you're leaving
In the morning, when you wake up
Leave me with some kind of proof it's not a dream

Ohh...

You are the only exception
You are the only exception
You are the only exception
You are the only exception
You are the only exception
You are the only exception
You are the only exception
You are the only exception

And I'm on my way to believing
Oh, And I'm on my way to believing

Where is the love?

The Black Eyed Peas

INFORMAÇÕES TÉCNICAS

Composição: The Black Eyed Peas and Justin Timberlake
Estilo: Dance, eletrônica, black music, pop, hip-hop
Integrantes da banda: Fergie, Will.I.am, apl.de.ap e Taboo
Site oficial: www.blackeyedpeas.com
Tema: Pacifista, antiguerra

Informações sobre a banda e a música

"Where is the love?", é o primeiro single de The Black Eyed Peas, do seu terceiro álbum, *Elephunk*, lançado em 16 de junho de 2003. Foi o primeiro single que contava com o novo membro do grupo, Fergie. A canção também tem a participação de Justin Timberlake nos vocais (refrão). Recebeu duas indicações para Gravação do Ano e de Melhor Rap/Sung Colaboração no Grammy Awards. Na música, The Black Eyed Peas lamenta por vários problemas no mundo. Muitos problemas são discutidos, como o terrorismo, a hipocrisia do governo dos EUA, racismo, guerras, intolerância e cobiça.

Teaching tips

Mostre o clipe oficial da música do Youtube sem o som.

Peça aos alunos que observem o clipe e descrevam o que veem. Pergunte a eles o que o cantor quer expressar nesse clipe. Eles devem escrever cinco palavras relacionadas ao clipe e em seguida observar o trecho. Em seguida, devem sublinhar os verbos no *present continuous* e também as palavras que rimam. Organize os alunos em duplas e peça a eles que discutam a estrofe. Na atividade seguinte eles vão ler a estrofe e responder às questões. Peça a eles que deem exemplos de fatos reais. Novamente devem procurar palavras que rimam.

Em seguida coloque a música e peça aos alunos que prestem atenção e tentem identificar cinco palavras com significado positivo e cinco com significado negativo. Compartilhe essas palavras com a classe toda. Em seguida, toque a música novamente e peça a eles que encontrem as palavras mencionadas na atividade. Os alunos devem escrever um parágrafo utilizando o maior número possível dessas palavras. No final da atividade, toque a música e cante com eles.

Para a atividade do *after listening*, peça que os alunos escolham uma estrofe, definindo-a como otimista ou pessimista. Em seguida, eles devem reescrevê-la com suas próprias palavras. Dependendo do perfil do seu grupo, os alunos podem fazer essa atividade somente ouvindo ou lendo a letra da música.

Answer key

Before listening

1. Violence, spray graffiti, unhappiness, doubts, love, end of times

2. *People killing, people dying*
   Children hurt and you hear them crying
   Can you practice what you preach?
   And would you turn the other cheek?

   Possible answer:
   There is a lot of violence in the world; children are surrounded by it. Can the people say what they think, are they able to question the government and accept the consequences?

3. a) Open answer. Suggestion: Children are influenced by the media because, first of all, they spend a lot of time in front of TV and computer. The lack of parent supervision allows them have access to things they are still not mature enough to understand. Children want to imitate their superheroes and sometimes do not realize the consequences.

b) *Wrong information always shown by the media*
   Negative images is the main criteria
   Infecting the young minds faster than bacteria
   Kids wanna act like what they see in the cinema

Listening

1. Positive: living, love, meditate, guidance, questions, information, truth, peace, values, fairness, faith
   Negative: bombs, killing, dying, addicted, trauma, suffering, insane, crying, terrorism, discriminate, badness, hurt.

2. Open answer.

3. Open answer.

4. Listen to the song and sing along.

After listening

1. Open answer.

Lyrics

"Where is the love?"

What's wrong with the world, mama?
People living like they ain't got no mamas
I think the whole world addicted to the drama
Only attracted to things that'll bring you trauma
Overseas, yeah, we try to stop terrorism
But we still got terrorists here living
In the USA, the big CIA
The Bloods and The Crips and the KKK
But if you only have love for your own race

Then you only leave space to discriminate
And to discriminate only generates hate
And when you hate then you're bound to get irate, yeah
Badness is what you demonstrate
And that's exactly how anger works and operates
Man, you gotta have love just to set it straight
Take control of your mind and meditate
Let your soul gravitate to the love, y'all, y'all
People killing, people dying
Children hurt and you hear them crying
Can you practice what you preach?
And would you turn the other cheek?
Father, Father, Father, help us
Send some guidance from above
'Cause people got me, got me questioning:
Where's the love? (Love)
Where's the love? (The love)
Where's the love? (The love)
Where's the love, the love, the love?
It just ain't the same
Always in change
New days are strange
Is the world insane?
If love and peace is so strong
Why are there pieces of love that don't belong?
Nations dropping bombs
Chemical gasses filling lungs of little ones
With ongoing suffering as the youth die young
So ask yourself:
Is the loving really gone?
So I could ask myself:
Really what is going wrong?
In this world that we living in
People keep on giving in
Making wrong decisions
Only visions of them dividends
Not respecting each other
Deny the brother

A war is going on

But the reason's undercover

The truth is kept secret

It's swept under the rug

If you never know truth

Then you never know love

Where's the love, y'all, come on

(I don't know)

Where's the truth, y'all, come on

(I don't know)

Where's the love, y'all

People killing, people dying

Children hurt and you hear them crying

Can you practice what you preach?

And would you turn the other cheek?

Father, Father, Father, help us

Send some guidance from above

'Cause people got me, got me questioning:

Where's the love? (Love)

Where's the love? (The love)

Where's the love? (The love)

Where's the love?

The love, the love

I feel the weight of the world on my shoulders

As I'm getting older, y'all, people gets colder

Most of us only care about money making

Selfishness got us following our wrong direction

Wrong information always shown by the media

Negative images is the main criteria

Infecting the young minds faster than bacteria

Kids wanna act like what they see in the cinema

Yo', whatever happened to the values of humanity

Whatever happened to the fairness in equality

Instead in spreading love we spreading animosity

Lack of understanding, leading lives away from unity

That's the reason why sometimes I'm feeling under

That's the reason why sometimes I'm feeling down

There's no wonder why sometimes I'm feeling under

Gotta keep my faith alive till love is found
Then ask yourself...
Where's the love?
Where's the love?
Where's the love?
Where's the love?
Father, Father, Father, help us
Send some guidance from above
'Cause people got me, got me questioning:
Where's the love?

Drops of Jupiter

Train

INFORMAÇÕES TÉCNICAS

Composição: Train

Estilo: Pop rock

Integrantes: Patrick Monahan (vocal), Jimmy Stafford (guitarra e vocal), Scott Underwood (bateria)

Site oficial: http://savemesanfrancisco.com/br/node/7398

Tema: Vida após morte

Informações sobre a banda e a música

Train é uma banda americana de pop rock de San Francisco, formada em 1994. "Drops of Jupiter" também é o título do segundo álbum (2001), responsável pela popularidade enorme da banda. Foi um *hit* international e ganhou dois Grammys em 2002.

A música "Drops of Jupiter" foi escrita por Patrick Monahan em homenagem à mãe, que morreu de câncer de pulmão por ser fumante. Monahan retornou a sua cidade natal, na Pensilvânia, e acordou uma manhã com as palavras "back in the atmosphere" em sua mente. Ao passar pela dor da perda, ele começou a compor a música. Monahan disse que a perda da pessoa mais importante na sua vida estava sempre em sua mente e o fez pensar: "e se ninguém nunca nos deixasse? E se a pessoa estivesse aqui mas de uma forma diferente?". Essa é a ideia na frase "back here in the atmosphere".

Teaching tips

Contextualize o assunto fazendo as perguntas do *Before listening*. Tenha certeza de que seu grupo tem a maturidade para conversar sobre esse tópico. Caso ache que o grupo não possa discutir dessa forma, informe que o compositor escreveu essa música para sua mãe que faleceu e passe para a atividade de *Listening*.

Antes da atividade, peça que façam, por escrito, um *brainstorming* sobre palavras conhecidas referentes a espaço e às estações do ano. Coloque a música para que verifiquem se escreveram alguma palavra que aparece na letra. Eles devem anotar todas as palavras referentes aos tópicos estação de ano ou espaço, responder à segunda pergunta do *Listening* e trocar ideias com os colegas. Em seguida peça a eles que completem as sentenças da atividade número 3, de maneira coerente. Eles podem compartilhar com os colegas as respostas. Em seguida toque a terceira estrofe da música e peça a eles que comparem as respostas com a letra da música. Nesse momento devem escutar a música e relacionar as sentenças na atividade seguinte. Na próxima atividade os alunos vão identificar na música os versos em que o cantor usa a expressão "tell me". Toque a música para que completem todas as sentenças que se iniciam com "tell me". Depois eles podem comparar em duplas.

Durante o *After listening*, peça a eles que conversem com um colega usando a expressão "tell me" para iniciar a conversa. Em seguida pergunte aos alunos se eles conhecem alguma outra música que abrange um tópico semelhante.

Answer key

Before listening

1. Open answer.

2. Open answer.

3. Open answer.

Listening

1. Atmosphere, Jupiter, Summer, drops, rain, time to change, moon, Spring, sun, milky way, heaven, shooting star, constellation, wind, Venus.

2. Suggestion:
   Because he believes his mother was travelling around Space and came back into the atmosphere.

3. Suggestions:
   Now that she's back <u>from the place she went.</u>
   Tracing her way <u>through the clouds again.</u>
   She checks out <u>if there is no one behind.</u>
   Reminds me <u>to be careful again.</u>
   Now that she's back <u>in my world again.</u>
   I'm afraid that <u>she might not want me anymore.</u>
   Plain old Jane <u>is what she will call me.</u>
   Who was too afraid <u>to speak before her.</u>

4. a) Now that she's back
   b) Tracing her way
   c) She checks out
   d) Reminds me
   e) Now that she's back
   f) I'm afraid that
   g) Plain old Jane
   h) Who was too afraid to

   (b) through the constellation
   (e) in the atmosphere
   (g) told a story about a man
   (c) Mozart while she does tae-bo
   (f) she might think of me as
   (h) fly so he never did land
   (a) from that soul vacation
   (d) that there's room to grow

5. Tell me, did you sail across the sun?
   Tell me, <u>did you fall from a shooting star?</u>
   Tell me, <u>did the wind sweep you off your feet?</u>
   Tell me, <u>did Venus blow your mind?</u>
   Tell me, <u>did you sail across the sun?</u>

After listening

1. Open answer.

2. Open answer.

Lyrics

"Drops of Jupiter"

Now that she's back in the atmosphere
With drops of Jupiter in her hair
She acts like summer and walks like rain
Reminds me that there's a time to change
Since the return of her stay on the moon
She listens like spring and she talks like June
But tell me, did you sail across the sun?
Did you make it to the milky way
To see the lights all faded
And that heaven is overrated
Tell me, did you fall from a shooting star?
One without a permanent scar
And did you miss me
While you were looking for yourself out there
Now that she's back from that soul vacation
Tracing her way through the constellation
She checks out Mozart while she does tae-bo
Reminds me that there's room to grow
Now that she's back in the atmosphere
I'm afraid that she might think of me as
Plain old Jane told a story about a man
Who was too afraid to fly so he never did land
But tell me, did the wind sweep you off your feet?
Did you finally get the chance to dance along the light of day
And head back to the milky way
And tell me, did Venus blow your mind?
Was it everything you wanted to find?
And did you miss me
While you were looking for yourself out there
Can you imagine, no love, pride, deep fried chicken
Your best friend always stick in up for you
(even when I know you're wrong)?
Can you imagine no first dance
Freeze dried romance

5 hour phone conversation
The best soy latte' that you ever had and...me?
But tell me, did the wind sweep you off your feet?
Did you finally get the chance to dance along the light of day
And head back toward the milky way?
Tell me, did you sail across the sun?
Did you make it to the milky way to see the lights all faded
And that heaven is overrated?
Tell me, did you fall for a shooting star?
One without a permanent scar?
And did you miss me while you were looking for yourself?
Nanananananananananananana
And did you finally get the chance to dance along the light of day?
And did you fall for a shooting star?
Fall for a shooting star?
And are you lonely looking for yourself out there?

Dear Mr. President

Pink

INFORMAÇÕES TÉCNICAS

Composição: Pink
Estilo: Pop punk, pop, rock, pop rock
Site oficial: www.pinkspage.com
Tema: Política

Informações sobre a cantora e a música

"Dear Mr. President" faz parte do quarto álbum da cantora Pink, *I'm not dead*, lançado em 2006. Pink disse que a música é uma carta aberta ao presidente dos Estados Unidos daquela época, George W. Bush, e que foi uma das músicas mais importantes que ela já escreveu.

Teaching tips

Organize a classe em duplas. Peça aos alunos que procurem na internet os deveres de um presidente de um país. Faça as perguntas do *Before listening*. Mostre o título da música e pergunte aos alunos quem a escreveu e por que. Coloque a música e peça a eles que prestem atenção na segunda e na terceira estrofes. Eles devem anotar as perguntas que Pink faz ao presidente dos Estados Unidos. Eles devem escutar toda a música, ler as sentenças da atividade 2 e responder com verdadeiro ou falso. Em seguida, é o momento de verificar as sentenças que Pink descreve na música como sendo um trabalho árduo. Nas atividades de *After listening* peça aos alunos que pesquisem na internet quais são os presidentes dos países citados. Eles podem discutir em duplas quais seriam seus pedidos se por acaso tivessem uma entrevista com o presidente do Brasil. Por fim, peça a eles que procurem quais foram os presidentes que ficaram menos tempo e mais tempo empossados aqui no Brasil e também nos Estados Unidos.

Answer key

Before listening

1. Research on the internet.

2. Open answer.

3. Open answer.

Listening

1. a) What do you feel when you see all the homeless on the street?
   b) Who do you pray for at night before you go to sleep?
   c) What do you feel when you look in the mirror?
   d) Are you proud?
   e) How do you sleep while the rest of us cry?
   f) How do you dream when a mother has no chance to say goodbye?
   g) How do you walk with your head held up high?
   h) Can you even look me in the eye and tell me why?

2. (T) If he is proud.
   (T) If he is lonely.
   (F) If he has a wife.
   (T) how he can take his daughter's rights away.

3. (x) Minimum wage with a baby on the way
   ( ) Working all day.
   (x) Rebuilding your house after the bombs took them away.
   ( ) Working with your gay daughter.
   (x) Building a bed out of a cardboard box.
   ( ) Working selling cocaine.

After listening

1. France: François Hollande (eleito em maio de 2012)
    United States: Barak Obama (eleito em 2008 e reeleito em 2012)
    Argentina: Cristina Kirchner (eleita em 2007 e reeleita em 2011)
    Chile: Sebastian Pinera (eleito em 2010)
    Germany: Joachim Gauck (assumiu em março de 2012, após renúncia de Christian Wulff)

2. Open answer.

3. United States
    Shortest: William Henry Harrison (served one month and died)
    Longest: Franklin D. Roosevelt (served 4422 days)

    Brazil
    Shortest: Carlos Luz (three days)
    Longest: Getúlio Vargas (18 years)

Lyrics

"Dear Mr. President"

Dear Mr. President
Come take a walk with me
Let's pretend we're just two people and
You're not better than me
I'd like to ask you some questions if we can speak
honestly

What do you feel when you see all the homeless on the street?
Who do you pray for at night before you go to sleep?
What do you feel when you look in the mirror?
Are you proud?

How do you sleep while the rest of us cry?
How do you dream when a mother has no chance to say goodbye?
How do you walk with your head held high?
Can you even look me in the eye?
And tell me why?

Dear Mr. President
Were you a lonely boy?
Are you a lonely boy?
Are you a lonely boy?
How can you say
No child is left behind?
We're not dumb and we're not blind
They're all sitting in your cells
While you pay the road to hell

What kind of father would take his own daughter's rights away?
And what kind of father might hate his own daughter if she were gay?
I can only imagine what the first lady has to say
You've come a long way from whiskey and cocaine

How do you sleep while the rest of us cry?
How do you dream when a mother has no chance to say goodbye?
How do you walk with your head held high?
Can you even look me in the eye?

Let me tell you about hard work
Minimum wage with a baby on the way
Let me tell you about hard work
Rebuilding your house after the bombs took them away
Let me tell you about hard work
Building a bed out of a cardboard box
Let me tell you about hard work
Hard work
Hard work
You don't know nothing about hard work
Hard work
Hard work

Oh

How do you sleep at night?
How do you walk with your head held high?
Dear Mr. President
You'd never take a walk with me
Would you?

If today was your last day

Nickelback

INFORMAÇÕES TÉCNICAS

Composição: Nickelback
Estilo: Rock
Integrantes: Chad Kroeger, Mike Kroeger, Ryan Peake e Brandon Kroeger
Site oficial: http://www.nickelback.com/
Tema: Vida

Informações sobre a banda e a música

Nickelback é uma banda de rock do Canadá formada em Hanna, em 1995. O nome da banda vem do *nickel* (moeda de cinco centavos canadense) que Mike Kroeger frequentemente tinha de dar de troco no seu trabalho numa cafeteria ("Here's your nickel back!").

Teaching tips

Mostre o título da música para os alunos e faça as perguntas do *Before listening* para contextualizar. Em seguida toque a música e peça a eles que ouçam somente a primeira estrofe e que escrevam quais os conselhos dados. Coloque a música novamente e peça que ordenem a terceira estrofe e a interpretem. Em seguida, eles devem ouvir a música toda e anotar todas as perguntas que iniciam com a palavra *would*. Na atividade 5 os alunos devem preencher os versos com as palavras que faltam e verificar quais são as palavras que rimam na estrofe.

Durante o *After listening* os alunos devem se sentar em duplas e responder às perguntas. Mostre a eles que estão desenvolvendo a habilidade de conversar usando o condicional.

Before listening

1. Open answer.

2. Open answer.

3. Open answer.

4. Open answer.

5. Open answer.

Listening

1. He said each day's a gift and not a given right
   Leave no stone unturned, leave your fears behind
   And try to take the path less traveled by
   That first step you take is the longest stride.

2. (4) *So live like you're never living twice*
   (1) *Against the grain should be a way of life*
   (3) *Every second counts 'cause there's no second try*
   (2) *What's worth the price is always worth the fight*
   (5) *Don't take the free ride in your own life*

3. Open answer.

4. a) Would you live each moment like your last?
   b) Would you call those friends you never see?
   c) Would you forgive your enemies?
   d) And would you find that one you're dreaming of?
   e) Would you make your mark by mending a broken heart?

5. And would you call those friends you never see?
   Reminisce old <u>memories</u>?
   Would you <u>forgive</u> your <u>enemies</u>?
   And would you find that one you're <u>dreaming</u> of?

<u>Swear</u> up and down to God above
That you'd finally <u>fall in love</u> if today was your last day?

see	of
memories	above
enemies	in love

After listening

1. Open answers.

Lyrics

"If today was your last day"

My best friend gave me the best advice
He said each day's a gift and not a given right
Leave no stone unturned, leave your fears behind
And try to take the path less traveled by
That first step you take is the longest stride

If today was your last day and tomorrow was too late
Could you say goodbye to yesterday?
Would you live each moment like your last
Leave old pictures in the past?
Donate every dime you had, if today was your last day?
What if, what if, if today was your last day?

Against the grain should be a way of life
What's worth the price is always worth the fight
Every second counts 'cause there's no second try
So live like you're never living twice
Don't take the free ride in your own life

If today was your last day and tomorrow was too late
Could you say goodbye to yesterday?
Would you live each moment like your last?
Leave old pictures in the past?
Donate every dime you had?

And would you call those friends you never see?
Reminisce old memories?
Would you forgive your enemies?
And would you find that one you're dreaming of?
Swear up and down to God above
That you'd finally fall in love if today was your last day?

If today was your last day
Would you make your mark by mending a broken heart?
You know it's never too late to shoot for the stars
Regardless of who you are

So do whatever it takes
'Cause you can't rewind a moment in this life
Let nothing stand in your way
'Cause the hands of time are never on your side

If today was your last day and tomorrow was too late
Could you say goodbye to yesterday?
Would you live each moment like your last?
Leave old pictures in the past?
Donate every dime you had?

And would you call those friends you never see?
Reminisce old memories?
Would you forgive your enemies?
And would you find that one you're dreaming of
Swear up and down to God above
That you'd finally fall in love if today was your last day?

Viva la vida

Coldplay

INFORMAÇÕES TÉCNICAS

Composição: Coldplay

Estilo: Rock

Integrantes da banda: Chris Martin (vocalista principal), Jonny Buckland guitarrista/ baixista, Will Champion (baterista, vocal de apoio e multi-instrumentista)

Site oficial: http://www.coldplay.com/

Tema: Religião

Informações sobre a banda e a música

Coldplay é uma banda britânica de rock alternativo fundada em 1996, na Inglaterra, pelo vocalista principal Chris Martin e o guitarrista Jonny Buckland no University College London. Depois de formar o Pectoralz, Guy Berryman se juntou ao grupo como baixista e eles mudaram o nome para Starfish. Will Champion entrou para tocar bateria, como vocal de apoio e multi-instrumentista, completando o grupo. Essa canção foi escrita por todos os membros da banda inglesa Coldplay e lançada em 2008.

A letra tem referências bíblicas e históricas. Ganhou o prêmio Canção do Ano no Grammy Awards em 2009. O nome da canção faz referência a uma pintura da artista mexicana Frida Kahlo.

Teaching tips

Inicie a aula conversando com seus alunos sobre a banda Coldplay. Pergunte o que sabem sobre ela, sua origem e quais músicas mais gostam. Introduza o tema de "Viva la vida" perguntando o quanto a religião faz parte de suas vidas. Organize a classe em duplas e peça aos alunos que respondam às primeiras perguntas. Em seguida eles devem compartilhar as respostas. Mostre o clipe uma primeira vez sem som. Peça aos alunos que observem os instrumentos que estão sendo usados pela banda. Mostre o clipe novamente (com som) ou toque a música para que completem a estrofe.

Toque novamente para os alunos ordenarem os versos. Em duplas eles vão discutir o significado dessa estrofe. Em seguida eles devem encontrar as estrofes que melhor exemplifiquem os três títulos. Toque uma terceira vez e peça aos alunos que tentem retirar as referências bíblicas da letra da música. Pergunte se alguém conhece alguma passagem bíblica correspondente.

Durante o *After listening*, os alunos vão ler as duas estrofes e preencher o quadro com as referências ao passado e ao presente. Peça a eles que interpretem o significado dos versos em duplas.

Answer key

Before listening

1. Open answers.

2. Drums, electric guitar, bass, violins, violas, cello, keyboard, percussion, harpsichord, cymbals.

Listening

1. *One minute I held the key*
    Next the walls were closed on me
    And I discovered that my castles stand
    Upon pillars of salt and pillars of sand.

2. (2) *I know Saint Peter won't call my name*
    (4) *But that was when I ruled the world*
    (1) *For some reason I can't explain*
    (3) *Never an honest word*

3. Suggestion:

    Saint Peter will not allow him to enter Heaven, maybe because he was not an honest man when he was a king or when he thought he could rule the world.

4. ***I built my power on unstable floor***
    One minute I held the key
    Next the walls were closed on me
    And I discovered that my castles stand
    Upon pillars of salt and pillars of sand

    I had the power but now there is no one by my side
    I used to rule the world
    Seas would rise when I gave the word
    Now in the morning I sleep alone
    Sweep the streets I used to own

    People always want the king's head
    Revolutionaries wait
    For my head on a silver plate
    Just a puppet on a lonely string
    Oh who would ever want to be king?

5. *Pillars of salt and pillars of sand*: Jesus talked about a wise man who built his house on the rocks and the silly one that built his house on the sand. Or it is an allusion to the Biblical story in which Lot's wife turned into a pillar of salt.

    Saint Peter won't call my name: Saint Peter at the entrance of Heaven.

    Seas would rise when I gave the word: Moses parted the Red sea.

After listening

1.

PAST	PRESENT
I used to rule the world	Now I sleep alone.
I gave the word	
I used to own (the streets)	I sweep the streets.
I used to roll the dice	
I used to feel the fear	
I listened as the crowd would sing	Now the old king is dead.

2. Open answers. Suggestion:
It's about being powerful and then losing the power.

Lyrics

"Viva la vida"

I used to rule the world
Seas would rise when I gave the word
Now in the morning I sleep alone
Sweep the streets I used to own
I used to roll the dice
Feel the fear in my enemy's eyes
Listened as the crowd would sing
"Now the old king is dead! Long live the king!"
One minute I held the key
Next the walls were closed on me
And I discovered that my castles stand
Upon pillars of salt and pillars of sand
I hear Jerusalem bells are ringing
Roman Cavalry choirs is singing
Be my mirror, my sword and shield
My missionaries in a foreign field
For some reason I can't explain

Once you'd gone there was never
Never an honest word
That was when I ruled the world
It was the wicked and wild wind
Blew down the doors to let me in
Shattered windows and the sound of drums
People couldn't believe what I'd become
Revolutionaries wait
For my head on a silver plate
Just a puppet on a lonely string
Oh who would ever want to be king?
I hear Jerusalem bells are ringing
Roman Cavalry choirs are singing
Be my mirror, my sword and shield
My missionaries in a foreign field
For some reason I can't explain
I know Saint Peter won't call my name
Never an honest word
But that was when I ruled the world
Oh, oh, oooh, oh, oh, oh(5x)
Hear Jerusalem bells are ringing
Roman Cavalry choirs are singing
Be my mirror, my sword and shield
My missionaries in a foreign field
For some reason I can't explain
I know Saint Peter won't call my name
Never an honest word
But that was when I ruled the world

Bibliografia

DOMONEY, L. & Harris, S. "Justified and ancient: Pop music in EFL classrooms". *ELT Journal*, 47, 1993, pp. 234-41.

EKEN, D. K. "Ideas for using songs in the English language classroom". English Teaching FORUM, 34/1:46-47, 1996.

LO, R. & Fai Li,H.C. "Songs enhance learner involvement". English Teaching FORUM, 36/3:8-11, 1998.

HORNER, D. Classroom ideas: songs and music. *MET*, 2/3, pp. 33-9, 1993.

LITTLE, J. "Pop and rock music in the ESL classroom". *TESL Talk*, 14, 1983, pp. 40-4.

Sobre as autoras

Louise Potter atua na área de ensino de língua estrangeira e treinamento de professores há mais de vinte anos; suas áreas de especialização são *teacher trainning* e *teacher development*. Comandou equipes de professores por doze anos em escola de idiomas e é autora de materiais didáticos para ensino de língua inglesa. É sócia-proprietária da Teach-in Education, empresa de capacitação e treinamento para professores de língua estrangeira.

Ligia Lederman é especialista em Linguística Aplicada ao Ensino de Língua Estrangeira pela UNICAMP, professora e autora de materiais didáticos de inglês, além de diretora e orientadora pedagógica de escola de idiomas.

Este livro foi composto nas fontes Milo e Milo Serif
e impresso em janeiro de 2013 pela Gráfica Vida e Consciência,
sobre papel offset 90g/m².